Ferdinand De Wilton Ward

Churches of Rochester

Ecclesiastical History of Rochester, N.Y.

Ferdinand De Wilton Ward

Churches of Rochester
Ecclesiastical History of Rochester, N.Y.

ISBN/EAN: 9783337098599

Printed in Europe, USA, Canada, Australia, Japan

Cover: Foto ©Lupo / pixelio.de

More available books at **www.hansebooks.com**

CHURCHES OF ROCHESTER.

ECCLESIASTICAL HISTORY

OF

ROCHESTER, N.Y.

NARRATIVE OF THE

RISE, PROGRESS, AND PRESENT CONDITION
OF EACH RELIGIOUS ORGANIZATION;

BIOGRAPHICAL SKETCHES OF

PASTORS, AND OF CLERGYMEN BORN IN
THE CITY;

WITH MISCELLANEOUS ITEMS,

FROM AUGUST, 1815, TO JULY, 1871.

BY

REV. F. DeW. WARD, D.D.,
OF GENESEO, N. Y.

ROCHESTER:
PUBLISHED BY ERASTUS DARROW,
OSBURN HOUSE BLOCK,
1871.

Entered, according to Act of Congress, in the year 1871, by

ERASTUS DARROW,

In the Office of the Librarian of Congress, at Washington.

REPUBLICAN PRESS: J. W. CLEMENT,
GENESEO, N. Y.

PREFACE.

WORKS BY REV. F. DeW. WARD, D. D., of Geneseo, N. Y.

INDIA AND THE HINDOOS.—Published by Messrs. Scribner & Co., New York; now out of print.

SUMMER VACATION ABROAD.—A journey through Britain, France, Italy, Belgium, &c., in 1854; Published by E. Darrow, Rochester. Price $1.09.

CHRISTIAN GIFT.—A Series of Letters addressed by a Pastor to young christains; published by E. Darrow, Rochester, N. Y.— Price 50 cents.

RELIGIOUS HISTORY OF ROCHESTER.—A Narrative of each Religious denomination of the City, from 1815 to 1871. Published by E. Darrow, Rochester. Price $1.00.

☞ Mailed on receipt of price, by

ERASTUS DARROW,
ROCHESTER, N. Y.

this a most unwelcome and unnnnnn soil. It has been the oft repeated expression that a religious history of Rochester be written to the glory of our common christianity, and as a grateful tribute to those who, under God, made the place what it is.

The writer of the following work little anticipated the time and labor that would be required in its prep-

REPUBLICAN PRESS: J. W. CLEMENT,
GENESEO, N. Y.

PREFACE.

For the reason that religion is the most important of all subjects, the ecclesiastical history of any community surpasses every other feature in value and true interest.

Rochester fitly attracts much attention by the rapidity of its growth — there being not a house in 1810 where the population now numbers 70,000 ; by its eminent position in regard to several articles of production, manufacture and commerce ; but especially by the high character it early secured, and has ever retained, for morality and religion. The founders of this "city of the wild" brought with them the Bible, and at once commenced those Sabbath and sanctuary services (preaching, prayer and sacraments) which had been their usage at their former homes. Atheism, Infidelity, with fatal religious heresies, have ever found this a most unwelcome and unfruitful soil. It has been the oft repeated expression that a religious history of Rochester be written to the glory of our common christianity, and as a grateful tribute to those who, under God, made the place what it is.

The writer of the following work little anticipated the time and labor that would be required in its preparation. Whatever success has attended the endeavor to save from oblivion important annals, and whatever interest the reader may find in perusing these pages, are largely due to the gentlemen who have rendered cheerful and abundant assistance. But for such aid the narratives had been meagre, incorrect and unsatisfactory, whereas there are now, it is believed, but few mistakes, and the omissions comparatively unimportant. The author presents his sincere thanks to present and former citizens — clerical and lay — for their many letters containing facts which find a place in these chapters. In the index, credit is given to contributors — the biographical sketches being almost entirely by the author. The three daily papers having obligingly published a notice many months ago of such a work in preparation, if any church is omitted, the fault rests with those who did not furnish information. The greatest difficulty has been in the spelling of proper names, especially those of foreign residents. Much assistance has been derived from C. C. Drew's admirable Directory for 1871, a copy of which was loaned by a friendly hand.

The last chapter contains facts and reminiscences interesting to many persons and worthy of historical preservation.

The printer, Mr. James W. Clement, of Geneseo, and the publisher, have done their best to render the volume attractive and acceptable to the reader.

Were the writer to make a formal dedication of his work, it would be to the MEMORY OF THE FOUNDERS OF CHRISTIAN CHURCHES IN THE VILLAGE AND CITY OF ROCHESTER.

INDEX.

	PAGES.
PREFACE......	3

PRESBYTERIAN.
General Introduction......	11
First......Seth H. Terry	13
Brick......Louis Chapin	25
Third......Dr. Hall's Anniversary Sermon	32
Central......Messrs. W. Alling and Geo. W. Parsons	39
Calvary......Rev. H. W. Morris	48
Saint Peter's......Edward A. Raymond	55
Westminster......Rev. Henry M. Morey	65
Reformed......Rev. R. D. Sproull	69
First United......Rev. James P. Sankey	71

EPISCOPALIAN.
Saint Luke's......Rev. Henry Anstice	76
Saint Paul's......Rev. J. V. VanIngen, D.D.	92
Trinity......Rev. C. H. W. Stocking	101
Christ's......Rev. Walton W. Battershall	112
Good Shepherd......Rev. Fred. W. Raikes	116

METHODIST.
All in one narrative, by Rev. D. W. C. Huntingdon, D.D.......	119

BAPTIST.
First......Wm. N. Sage	133
Second......D. R. Barton	140
German......Rev. Earnest Tschirch	144

CONGREGATIONAL.
First......Samuel D. Porter	149
Free Church......O'Reilly's History	150
Plymouth......Erastus Darrow	151

INDEX.

SINGLE CHURCHES.

Zion's First Evangelical Lutheran..........Rev. F. VonRosenberg 159
German United Evangelical...........Rev. Charles Siebenpfeiffer 158
First German Evangelical Association.........Rev. Michael Lehn 160
First English Lutheran.......................Rev. Reuben Hill 161
Evangelical Reformed Emanuel..............Rochester Directory 162
Evangelical Saint Paul's.................... " " 162
First Reformed (Dutch)........... ....Rev. P. Bahler 163
First Universalist....................Rev. George Montgomery 164
First Unitarian..............................D. L. Crittenden 165
Roman Catholic...................Catholic and City Directories 167
Friends..............................O'Reilly and Directory 169
Jews ....Directory 170
Second Advent.............................Directory 170

YOUNG MEN AND THE MINISTRY........ 173

MISCELLANY.

Preferments of Rochester Pastors 176
Long Pastorates.............. 177
Desirable Changes of Use........................ 177
Revivals 178
The Bible... 179
Foreign Missions.. 180
Tracts and Books.................... 180
Sabbath Schools..... 180
Temperance 181
Fires 182
Benevolent and Christian Institutions.... 183
University of Rochester.................................... 183
Rochester Theological Seminary........ 184
Rapid Church Erection..................................... 184
Fall of a Steeple.. 184

Explanations, Errata, and Additions,

Which Readers are requested to notice as they peruse the Volume.

It was originally intended to embody in this work biographical sketches of pioneer citizens who have taken an active and prominent part in organizing and establishing the various churches. Limited room and difficulty of selection have rendered unadvisable this interesting feature. Such narratives would form in themselves a valuable and welcome volume. The 1,500 different persons herein named include most of the early christian comers.

SABBATH SCHOOLS.—In addition to the statements on page 180, the following, furnished by Louis Chapin, Esq., are of great historic value: "In 1870 Rochester had 50 Protestant Sunday schools, 1,353 teachers, 12,410 scholars, with an average attendance of 8,674. During that year, 429 persons connected with these Sunday schools, united with the various churches on profession of their faith."

FIRST PRESBYTERIAN.—Add to "Summary," the names of *Elders* R. M. Dalzel, E. W. Armstrong, M.D., and John W. Adams. Also, Dr. Penney not Penny, Glasgow not Glascow, font not fount.

THIRD PRESBYTERIAN.—Died, in Rochester, Sept. 10, 1871, Rev. A. G. Hall, D.D , the pastor for thirty-one years of the Third Presbyterian church.

"Servant of Christ—well done—
Rest from thy loved employ."

SAINT PETER'S, PRESBYTERIAN.—A chime of nine bells placed in the tower in 1860, were melted in the fire of 1868, but replaced by a chime of twelve bells upon rebuilding the structure. Page 59, fourth line from top, for Rev. Dr. Hall read Rev. W. H. Green, D.D., of Princeton, N. J. Page 61, third line from bottom, for Chicago read Bridgeport, Conn.

viii EXPLANATIONS, ERRATA, AND ADDITIONS.

SAINT LUKE'S, EPISCOPAL.—Page 83, eighteenth line from top, for "early decree," read "academic degree." *Wardens* in succession—Nathaniel Rochester, 1817-19; Samuel I. Andrews, '17-20; Geo. G. Sill, '20; William Atkinson, '20-22; J. Mastick, '22-6; W. Pitkin, '27-66; S. O. Smith, '28-33; V. Matthews, '34-46; N. T. Rochester, '47-58, and '66-68; W. Brewster, 1859, and G. H. Perkins from 1869. *Vestrymen* have been from almost all the leading members. *Clerks of Vestry*—R. Babbitt, 1817-21; N. T. Rochester, '21-33, and '35-43; H. E. Rochester, '32-33 and '44; E. D. Smith, '34; T. C. Montgomery, '45-54; F. A. Whittlesey, '55-56 and '62; J. A. Eastman, '57-61; P. W. Garfield, '63-64; E. A. Frost, '65; R. H. Rochester, '65-66; J. P. Humphrey, '66; Allen Ayrault, H. L. Churchill, '67-69; W. Eastwood, '70; T. Raines, '71. *Treasurers*—R. Babbitt, '17-21; N. T. Rochester, '22-32; W. Pitkin, '32-36; F. Whittlesey, '36-39; C. Morse, '39-44; I. M. Fish, '44; H. Scranton, '45-48; A. J. Brackett, '49-54; E. Whalen, '55-62; A. Karnes, '62-65; E. R. Hammatt, '65 (These were reluctantly left out in the following narrative for want of space in that position).

FIRST BAPTIST.—Page 135, for Geo. Davison read Geo. Dawson, and for Richard M. Scott read Richard M. Nott. Page 138, for Ezra Owen read Ezra Zeburn. Treasurer, E. T. Oatley. This church has a flourishing out-station entitled The Rapids Mission chapel, which promises an useful future to the southern part of the city.

SECOND BAPTIST.—In 1870 this church established a mission and built a handsome and commodious chapel on the corner of East avenue and Anson Park, at a cost of $18,000; the lot cost $5,000. It is named Bethlehem Mission. A Sabbath school of 250 scholars, under the superintendence of Mr. J. S. Phillips, meet in the chapel on the Sabbath, and a meeting for worship is held on Tuesday evening.

Aristarchus Champion, Esq., whose name often appears in the following pages, died in Rochester on the 18th of September, 1871, at the advanced age of ninety years. A native of Connecticut, he had made his home in this place since 1826. He possessed abundant wealth, which he devoted largely to the cause of morality and religion.

PRESBYTERIAN.

GENERAL INTRODUCTION.

In the spring of 1813, the population of Rochester (then a part of the town of Gates), consisted of about eight or ten families. As late as January of that year heathen worship was celebrated, and for the last time, by the Seneca Indians, on the occasion of their annual feast. This occurred on the spot where the Erie canal intersects with South Washington street, at the north-west corner, where the old Bethel church stood. The public worship of God on the Sabbath was then first held at the instance of Mrs. Hamlet Scrantom and Mrs. Wheelock, "women of faith and prayer," who obtained from Mr. Jehiel Barnard permission to use the upper story of his tailor shop on Buffalo street for that purpose. This shop stood on the north side of the street, and not far east from State street, a little west of the present entrance to the "Arcade." The room for worship was twenty-two feet long and fourteen wide. Mr. Barnard (who subsequently married the daughter of Mrs. Scrantom, and whose marriage was the first one celebrated in Rochester) and Mr. Warren Brown conducted the meetings, the exercises of which were extempore prayer, singing, and reading a sermon.

After some months the Rev. Daniel Brown, a Baptist minister of Pittsford, and Rev. Reuben Parmelee, a Presbyterian minister of Victor, came occasionally and preached to the people, who were then worshipping in the lower room of Mr. Barnard's building, used also as a school room. From that time down to August, 1815, there was but one place of worship for all denominations—first, Mr. Barnard's shop; and afterwards, as early as May, 1814, a small school house (then just built) on the spot where now stands the Free Academy.

The first movement for separation was made in August, 1815. This separation was amicable, and those of different religious tenets assisted each other afterwards in the building of their original houses of worship, and in the support of a preached gospel.

FIRST CHURCH.

The Presbytery of Geneva, shortly prior to August 22, 1815, appointed a committee, to meet at Rochester (then a part of Gates) on the day last named, to take into consideration the expediency of forming a church. The committee consisted of Rev. Daniel Fullar and Rev. Reuben Parmelee, ministers; Deacon Samuel Stone and Deacon Isaac B. Barnum, elders. They convened on the day appointed. Rev. Eleazer Fairbanks and Rev. Comfort Williams being present, were invited to sit in council. Rev. Mr. Fullar was chosen moderator, and Rev. Mr. Parmelee scribe.

"Articles of Faith," fourteen in number; "Articles of Practice," twelve in number; and a "Covenant," were submitted and adopted by Oliver Gibbs, Daniel West, Henry Donelly, Elisha Ely, Warren Brown, Charles Magne, Aaron Lay, Jane Gibbs, Elizabeth West, Hannah Donelly, Hannah Ely, Huldah Stoddard, Polly Magne, Sarah Lay, Sybil Bickford, Arabella Starks, who, having professed their faith according to said articles and entered into said covenant, were constituted into a regular church of Christ.

Oliver Gibbs and Daniel West were chosen elders, with the designation of deacons; and Warren Brown and Henry Donelly were chosen elders. These men were ordained and set apart to their offices by prayer and a charge agreeably to the Directory of the Presbyterian church. The population of Rochester was then 331.

Of the original members of the church, one only, Mrs. Polly Magne, of Baltimore, Md., is now living.

Rev. Comfort Williams was installed as first pastor, January 17, 1816, in an unfinished store on Carroll (now State) street; the ministers officiating being Rev. Messrs. A. C. Collins, J. Merrill, E. Fitch, D.D., Wm. Clark, R. Parmelee, J. H. Hotchkin, and F. Pomeroy —all deceased. Such was the sparseness of the population that a meeting of the church could not be regularly convened unless "notice had been sent to settlements on the ridge in Gates and in the east part of Brighton." After a pastorate of nearly four years, Mr. Williams resigned, May 11, 1821, and was succeeded by Rev. Joseph Penny, who was installed April 3, 1822, holding the position with marked ability and acceptance till April 16, 1833, when at his own request the pastorate relation was dissolved.

The records of the church contain the following entry: "NOTE.—Public worship was constantly maintained and kept up from the dismission of Rev. Mr. Williams until the settlement of Mr. Penny. It was so directed by Divine Providence that there was preaching every Sabbath during the whole time, excepting two whole and two half days, at which times service was attended and sermons read. So certain of having preaching did some individuals feel as not to have doubts about it when no minister had come so late as Saturday night, and though they had heard of none that was expected. So careful was a most merciful Redeemer to take care and feed the little flock, which was not only seemingly without a teacher, but encompassed with great difficulties, dangers and distresses, both from within and without."

Rev. Tryon Edwards was installed pastor July 2, 1834, and was succeeded, May 19, 1845, by Rev. Malcom N. McLaren, D.D., whom ill health compelled to resign in two years, when Rev. Joshua H. McIlvaine, D.D., assumed the pastorate, and was followed (May, 1861) by Rev. Calvin Pease, D.D., whose lamented death occurred in Vermont, September 17, 1863. The charge was then assumed by Rev. Caspar M. Wines, who held the same from May 22, 1866, to July, 1868, when he removed to the east, and was succeeded by Rev. J. L. Robertson, the present incumbent, who was installed the eighth pastor, September 15, 1870, and who is laboring with much efficiency and success among an attached people.

The original church edifice—a plain wooden building standing on piers—was erected on State (then Carroll) street, where is now Hamilton's block. To meet the demands of a rapidly increasing population and multiplying Sabbath assemblage, a lot was secured in the rear of the court house, where was erected a stone structure of ample and attractive appearance, which was dedicated to the worship of God October 28, 1824. A discourse preached upon the occasion by the pastor, Rev. Joseph Penny, D.D., attracted much attention, and was widely circulated over the land. Repeated enlargements and improvements were made in the building, until it was so much injured by a fire that entire reconstruction became an imperative necessity. Before this occurrence, the lecture room on the east side of the edifice had been removed, and one of large size and architectural beauty erected on the west side. The ground, being greatly needed for public purposes, was sold to the city, and a lot has been purchased on the corner of Plymouth avenue and Spring street, upon which a new edifice is in course of erection, the corner-stone having been laid with appropriate services.

The "old First" has a history of rare interest. Sermons of great power have been preached, and scenes of surpassing importance have been witnessed, within its walls. Of many now on earth, and more in the heavenly world, may it be said, "This and that man was born there." Never will that spot be forgotten by the many who there made for the first time public profession of their faith in Jesus; there received their first communion; there brought their children to the baptismal fount; and there listened to funeral discourses commemorating the lost of heart and home. An historian may not indulge in sentiment, therefore the writer must refrain from expressing emotions awakened by what that building has been to him and his for two score years.

We pass from the building with its deeply interesting associations to notice the

PASTORS OF THE FIRST.

Rev. Comfort Williams was a native of Wethersfield, Conn.; graduated at Yale and Andover; commenced his ministry at Ogdensburgh, N. Y., removing to this (then) village, and took the pastoral charge of this church January 17, 1816 (the sermon being preached by Rev. Dr. Fitch, first president of Williams college, Mass.), being dismissed, at his own request, May 11, 1821. To be the first religious instructor in a community like this is to occupy a position of special honor and responsibility. The name of "Parson Williams" lives in but few living memories, for pastor and people have, with few exceptions, gone to their eternal rest. A street on the east side of the river (Comfort street) perpetuates his name and home. A son, Charles H. Williams, still resides in the city.

Rev. Joseph Penny, D.D., was born in Ireland; educated in Dublin and Glascow; migrated to this country, accompanied by Rev. John Mulligan, in 1819; resided a brief time at Jamaica, L. I.; was installed pastor of this church April 3, 1822; resigned April 16, 1833; assumed charge of the First Congregational church of Northampton, Mass., from which he soon passed to the presidency of Hamilton college, N. Y., where he remained four years. After a temporary residence at Nyack, N. Y., and Grand Rapids, Mich., Dr. Penny returned to this city, and after years of intense suffering from a nervous affection (during which period his wife and her sister, Miss Sterling, both died), he "fell asleep in Jesus" March 22, 1860, and lies entombed on Mount Hope, beside many members of his cherished household. Of masculine intellect, large scholastic attainments, commanding presence, a warm Irish heart, and unusual facility of conversation, Dr. Penny has left an ineffaceable impression upon this community and region. Whatever aimed to advance the people, intellectually as well as religiously, received his cordial sympathy and earnest coöperation. His portrait, purchased by public contribution, graces the Athenæum, of which valued institution (under its original title of the "Franklin Institute") he was a leading projector. When he assumed the presidency of Hamilton college, gentlemen of this city became responsible for his salary for ten years. His published discourses—entitled "The House of Mirth," "Address at the Laying of the Corner-stone of the First Church," "Dedication Discourses," "Fourth of July Oration," and "Installation of Rev. Messrs. Ward and Cherry as Missionaries to India"—are models of thought and expression, indicating power and cultivation. His early, life-long and gifted friend, Mr. Mulligan, was for a considerable period one of the most popular teachers in western New York, and at the time of his death, in 1860, was principal of a large seminary at the metropolis. The life career of these gifted sons of Erin began, continued and ended almost simultaneously. "In death they were not divided."

Rev. Tryon Edwards, D.D., was born in Hartford, Conn.; graduated at Yale and Princeton, and became third pastor of the First church July 2, 1834. Resigning in 1844, he removed to New London, Conn., and ministered to a large Congregational society, from which place he removed to Hagerstown, Md., where he still resides, holding at the same time the presidency of the Wilson Female seminary, having been active in its establishment and prosperity. Enjoying and improving the advantages of our best seminaries of literature and theology, with a mind well and successfully trained to habits of thought and expression, his discourses (especially a series addressed to young men), coupled with courteous manners out of the pulpit, made him popular while a resident here, and will give him a long continued place in the memory of those who attended his ministry and enjoyed his acquaintance during his ten years pastorate of this church.

Rev. Malcolm N. McLaren, D.D., a native of Albany, N. Y.; graduated at Union and Princeton, and after ministering in several places, came to Rochester in 1845; after two years pastorate he resigned to assume charge of a Dutch Reformed church at Brooklyn, which he subsequently left and removed to Newburgh, from whence he came to Caledonia, where he now ministers to a large and important community. Wherever located, Dr. McLaren has always commanded universal respect for superior qualities, in and out of the pulpit; securing attention to the truth by clear and eloquent exhibition of doctrine and duty, heightened in effect by marked courtesy of manner, and a warm heart.

Rev. Joshua H. McIlvaine, D.D., was born in Delaware; studied at Princeton college and seminary; was pastor of a Presbyterian church at Little Falls, then at Utica (Westminster); coming to Rochester April 23, 1848, where he presided over the First with great ability till his removal to the chair of Political Economy and Rhetoric in his *alma mater*, which he has recently left to become pastor of the High Street church at Newark, N. J. In native talents, studious investigation, thorough scholarship, nervous expression, and pulpit power, Dr. McIlvaine has few equals among the thinkers, students, authors and preachers of the land or age. He is in middle life, and has before him a hopeful future of honor and usefulness.

Rev. Calvin Pease, D.D., was of New England origin, his parents being of Puritan faith, tradition and habits. The place of his birth was Canaan, Conn., and his scholastic graduation at the University of Vermont, of which institution he subsequently became professor and president. In May, 1861, he was installed pastor of this church, holding the position with increasing popularity and enlarging usefulness until his lamented death, when on a visit to Burlington, on the 17th of September, 1863. Says an intimate acquaintance, "In him, as I think, Vermont has lost her ablest man, one who combined the highest, most exact and critical scholarship, the most liberal and far-reaching views, the greatest practical ability with an intuitive perception of the characteristic qualities of men he came in contact with." These traits were happily illustrated during his brief but memorable pastorate here. A committee was sent to represent the church at the funeral, and testimonials of affection were presented to the widow and her family. The death of Dr. Pease was no common affliction, and his returnless absence no common loss to this city and region.

Rev. Caspar Maurice Wines, son of E. C. Wines, D.D., widely and favorably known in connection with prison reform, was born in Philadelphia, educated at

Washington College, Pennsylvania, and Princeton Theological Seminary. After temporary ministrations in Jersey City and Newburgh, he became pastor of the First church March 22, 1866, which position he held for two years with much ability. He has since preached to congregations at Brookline, Mass., and is now pastor of a church in Hartford, Conn.

Rev. James L. Robertson was born at Steubenville, Ohio, of Scotch parents; pursued his classical studies at Northwood, Ohio (Ref. Pres. Coll., now extinct), and theological in Allegheny, Pa. Having been licensed by the Presbytery of Steubenville, he was ordained and installed pastor of the United Presbyterian church of Geneva, N. Y., from which he passed to the pastoral charge of the Second Presbyterian church of Cincinnati, Ohio, and thence to the First Presbyterian church of Rochester, over which he was installed pastor December 7, 1870.

ELDERS AND DEACONS.

The following have been elected and ordained elders of the church. The dates of their ordination are given:

August 22, 1815—Oliver Gibbs, Daniel West, Warren Brown, Henry Donnelly.

July 7, 1816—Azel Ensworth.

August 4, 1822—Jacob Gould, Levi Ward, Jr.

July 18, 1824—Russell Green, Moses Chapin, Salmon Scofield.

January 27, 1828—Charles J. Hill, Frederick Starr.

April 21, 1833—Ashley Sampson, James K. Livingston.

April 29, 1839—Charles W. Dundas, Marcus Holmes.

August 2, 1846—Robert M. Dalzell, Eben N. Buell.

June 10, 1849—Edward W. Armstrong, Charles Church, Thomas Kempshall.

May 20, 1855—John W. Adams, James S. Tryon, George Dutton.

February 25, 1863—Oliver M. Benedict, Seth H. Terry.

January 8, 1871—William Burke, Seth H. Terry, Charles J. Hayden, Oscar Craig.

Of the above there are still living, Mr. Hill, who is now a member of Plymouth Congregation church in this city; Mr. Livingston, who lives at Newark, N. J.; Mr. Dundas, at Baltimore, Md.; Mr. Tryon, at Hartford, Conn.; Mr. Buell, in Rochester; besides Messrs. Dalzell, Armstrong, Adams, Benedict, Terry, Burke, Hayden, and Craig, who are the present acting elders. Mr. Craig is clerk of the session.

The following have been elected and ordained Deacons of the church:

August 22, 1815—Oliver Gibbs, Daniel West.

August 4, 1822—Levi Ward, Jr.

February 2, 1850—John G. Dabney, William Burke.

January 8, 1871—John T. Fox, James F. Baker.

THE SABBATH SCHOOL SUPERINTENDENTS

Have been, from 1817 to 1826, inclusive, Messrs. Elisha Ely, Everard Peck, David W. Allen, John H. Thompson, Ashley Sampson, and Josiah Bissell, Jr.

1827 to 1829—Charles J. Hill.

1829 to 1831—Ashley Sampson.

1831 to 1833—Charles J. Hill.
1834 to 1836—Walter S. Griffith.
1837 to 1852—L. A. Ward.
1852 to 1856—John N. Pomeroy.
1856 to 1858—John W. Adams.
1858 to 1862—Rev. J. H. McIlvaine, D.D.
1862 to 1868—O. M. Benedict.
1868 to present time—George C. Buell.

MINISTERS AND MISSIONARIES FROM THIS CHURCH.

Jonathan S. Green, S. Islands.
F. DeW. Ward, D.D., India; Geneseo.
Henry Cherry, India; South.
T. Dwight Hunt, S. Islands; California.
James Ballantine, Rochester.
L. Merrill Miller, D.D., Ogdensburgh.
Henry E. Peck, deceased.
Charles G. Lee, deceased.
Frederick M. Starr, deceased.
Everard Kempshall, D.D., Elizabeth, N. J.
William N. McCoon.
Charles R. Clarke, San Diego.
Henry B. Chapin, Ph. D., New York City.
Robert Proctor.
George Dutton, deceased.
M. L. R. P. Hill, Gloversville, N. Y.
G. Parsons Nichols, Milwaukee.
Henry A. DeForest, M.D., Syria, deceased.
Mrs. DeForest, Syria.
Mrs. Delia Stone Bishop, S. Islands.
Mrs. Maria Ward Chapin Smith, Syria, deceased.

SUMMARY, JULY 1, 1871.

Pastor—Rev. James L. Robertson.

Elders—Oliver M. Benedict, Seth H. Terry, William Burke, Charles J. Hayden, and Oscar Craig (clerk of session).

Deacons—Joshua T. Fox and James Baker.

Sabbath School Superintendent—George C. Buell.

Sabbath School Pupils—275.

Communicants—475.

SECOND (OR BRICK) CHURCH.

This Society was organized November 18th, 1825, with twenty-five members, of whom three only are now living, viz: Aurelia Gorsline (still a communicant), Derick Sibley (residing at Cincinnati, Ohio), and Seth Case (at Glenbula, Wisconsin). The first place of worship was a frame building on the west side of (Carroll, now) State street. A brick structure on the corner of Fitzhugh and (Ann, now) Allen streets was completed in 1828, which was used till April 1st, 1860, when it was closed with appropriate and impressive exercises, its place being taken by the present commodious edifice, which was dedicated June 30th, 1861; the sermon being preached by Rev. Samuel Fisher, D.D., then President of Hamilton College.

The corporate name of the church was changed November 10, 1833, from the "Second" to the "Brick Presbyterian Church in Rochester," and so reported to Presbytery February, 1834.

A Sunday School was organized at an early period, but no records are to be found prior to 1827, at which time there were seven teachers and thirty-nine scholars with a library of eight bound volumes and a few tracts.

In August, 1844, when the Washington street (now

the Central) church needed and asked help, fifteen valuable members of the Brick, mostly with families, responded to the call and joined them. Upon the organization of the Plymouth (Congregational) church, in 1855, thirteen communicants went there.

This church has been blessed with frequent revivals, which added to its membership, between 1826 and 1870, two thousand two hundred and thirty-one upon profession of their faith. The largest additions were in 1831, 100; 1832, 208; 1834, 200; 1843, 118; 1844, 83; 1837, 111; 1861, 68; 1864, 67; 1862, 207; 1869, 74.

A memorial chapel is now erecting by members of this parish on the corner of Hudson and Wilson streets, at an outlay of $10,000 or more.

PASTORS.

The first pastor, Rev. William James, D.D., was born at Albany, N. Y., in 1807; graduated at Princeton, N J., college and Theological seminary; preached for a brief time at Clarkson, N. Y.; assumed the pastorate of the Brick church, April, 1826, and resigned in 1830; became for a few months pastor of the Third Presbyterian church of Albany, N. Y., and, after a protracted illness, died in his native city on the 15th of February, 1868. Among his last utterances were these: "It is all joy—joy—joy!" "My faith is perfect, is perfect." "The other side is all sunshine." "I am ready to shout at the vision of the exceeding glory." "Nothing is so precious to me as that Christ died for us." For richness of thought, and power of expression, and eloquence of utterance, Dr. James has had few equals among the pulpit orators of the land. His published discourses, entitled the "Debt of nations to Christianity" and "The Moral responsibility of the American nation," were delivered in this city, and are well entitled to preservation in print.

During the year following the resignation of Dr. James the pulpit was supplied by Rev. Daniel N.✗ Merrit, and Rev. F. DeW. Ward, then under appointment as a missionary to India.

The second pastor, Rev. Wm. Wisner, D.D., was born at Warwick, N. Y., commenced the practice of law, and, after a course of private instruction, was licensed to preach the Gospel. His first pastorate was at Ithaca, N. Y., which he left to take charge of the Brick church in this city. Arriving here in 1831, he remained four years, when he went to St. Louis, but soon returned to his early home in Ithaca, and closed a long, honored and useful life at Cedar Rapids, Iowa, January 7, 1861. During his pastorate of this church, a debt of $14,000 was paid; the edifice underwent extensive repairs; the membership largely increased, his able and faithful ministrations being crowned with abundant success. Dr. Wisner and his son, Dr. W. C. Wisner, of Lockport, have both been Moderators of General Assembly.

The third pastor was Rev. George Beecher, son of the late Rev. Lyman Beecher, D.D., who was installed June 28, 1838, and resigned October 6, 1840. He then removed to Chilicothe, Ohio, where he accidentally shot himself, July 1, 1843. His memoirs have been written by his sister.

Fourth in the pastorate of this church is the present

✗ David Nye Merrit.

incumbent, Rev. James Boylen Shaw, D.D. Born in New York city, he became a member of the Brick church (now on Murray Hill). He was one of the first children upon whose head the venerable Dr. Spring laid his hands in baptism. Upon completing a classical education in his native city, and theological at Auburn, he became pastor of the Presbyterian church at Attica, from whence he removed to this city in December, 1840. For thirty-one years has Dr. Shaw prosecuted his ministry here with a fidelity and success seldom equalled. He has seen results of his labors far beyond what is usually permitted to the most favored. He was Moderator of the General Assembly in 1865, at Brooklyn, having been elected by acclamation.

THE RULING ELDERS

Of this church have been, Messrs. Timothy L. Bacon, Linus Stevens, Silas Hawley (1825), Worthington Wright, Benjamin Campbell (1827), Enos Pomeroy (1832), Orlando Hastings, David Dickey, John H. Thompson (1833), James Seymour, Jacob M. Schermerhorn, Harvey Pratt (1838), Jeremiah Hildreth, Samuel W. Lee, H. C. Fenn, Edwin Scrantom (1846), Louis Chapin, Richard Gorsline, J. W. Hatch, Edwin T. Huntingdon, Truman A. Newton, and Jacob Howe (1859). Of these officers eleven are deceased, four resigned, and seven now acting.

THE DEACONS

Have been Messrs. Abner Hubbard, Phineas B.

Cook, Charles W. Dundas (1833), Edward Bardwell, David O. Porter, John T. Fox, and Charles J. Hayden, of whom one is deceased, four dismissed by letter, and two acting.

THE SUNDAY SCHOOL.

Has always been an important adjunct and cooperative agency of this church. The superintendents have been Messrs. Jonathan Brown (1827), John H. Thompson (*twenty-three years*), Alex. J. Burr (1838), Samuel W. Lee (1840), Nelson Hall (1842-3), Louis Chapin (1847, '65-6), Richard Dibble (1849), James F. Conklin (1850), Edwin T. Huntington (1854-8), Truman A. Newton (1862-4), Jesse W. Hatch (1867), and Elisha M. Carpenter (1868-9-70).

During the last forty-three years there have been received into the church from the Sabbath school, upon profession of their faith, *one hundred and twenty-four teachers, and one thousand and sixty-five scholars.*

MEMBERS OF THE BRICK WHO HAVE ENTERED THE MINISTRY.

Rev. David C. Ames.
Rev. Horace H. Allen, Oneonta, N. Y.
Rev. Charles R. Burdick, Joilet, Ill.
Rev. Lemuel Clark.
Rev. Philo G. Cook, Buffalo, N. Y.
Rev. Darwin Chichester, Hammondsport, N. Y.
Rev. Nathan Chapin, La Crosse, Wis.
Rev. Elisha M. Carpenter, New York city.

Rev. Hiram W. Congdon.
Rev. David Dickey, Bethel Society, Rochester.
Rev. W. Evarts.
Rev. Corlis B. Gardner, Cuba, N. Y.
Rev. T. Dwight Hunt, Niles, Michigan.
Rev. Aug. F. Hall, died at Webster, N. Y.
Rev. Parsons C. Hastings, Brooklyn (a merchant).
Rev. Gavin L. Hamilton, Rochester.
Rev. Alvan Ingersoll, died at Rochester, 1863.
Rev. Thomas H. Johnson, Rehoboth, Mass.
Rev. Jonathan Ketchum.
Rev. Amos D. McCoy.
Rev. David Millard.
Rev. George W. Mackie, Chicago, Ill.
Rev. Enoch K. Miller, Texas.
Rev. Henry T. Miller.
Rev. James S. Pierpont, San Francisco, Cal.
Rev. James H. Phelps, Flushing, Mich.
Rev. David H. Palmer, Prattsburg, N. Y.
Rev. John Spink, Methodist.
Rev. Augustus C. Shaw (son of the pastor), Fulton, N. Y.
Rev. Edwin S. Wright, D.D., Fredonia, N. Y.
Rev. Ansley D. White, Clinton, Ill.
Rev. Worthington Wright.

SUMMARY, JULY 1, 1871.

Pastor.—Rev. James Boylen Shaw, D.D.

Elders—Messrs. David Dickey, Harvey C. Fenn, Edwin Scrantom, Louis Chapin, Jesse W. Hatch, Edwin T. Huntington, and Truman A. Newton.

Deacons—Messrs. Edward Bardwell and David O. Porter.

S. S. Superintendent—Edwin T. Huntington.

Teachers—72.   *Scholars*—822.

Church Communicants—1250.

MEMORIAL CHAPEL.

This recent erection, located on the north-east corner of Hudson and Nelson streets, derived its name from the fact that members of the Brick church contributed their proportion of the monies donated by them during the memorial years of 1869 and 1870, to this their colony. Commenced as a Sabbath school held in a public school house number eighteen, it has become a separate body, under the Rev. Gavin L. Hamilton, who had ministered for a period at Pittsford, and who, on the first of January, 1871, took hold of this enterprise with an earnestness, ensuring under God, large results for good in a locality needing the labors of a faithful pastor and working church. May the child be worthy of the parent. More can hardly be asked.

ERRATA IN

Page 25, eleventh line from bottom, Samuel W. Fisher.

Page 25, eighth line from bottom, in Rochester.

Page 27, fourteenth line from bottom

Page 28, eighth line from bottom

THIRD CHURCH.

In December, 1826, a religious society was incorporated on the east side of the river (then called Brighton), which ultimately became the "Third Presbyterian church of Rochester." The first place of worship was a school house on the corner of Mortimer and Clinton streets. This being too strait for the congregation, a building was erected on the same street, size 24 by 60, the timber standing in its native forest on Monday and services held on the next Lord's day. As if to add to the celebrity of this structure, within its walls originated the plan, which was afterwards adopted by the American Bible society, of supplying every destitute family in the land with a copy of the word of God; and also that honest but abortive effort to prevent by law of Congress the transportation of the mail and to close all post-offices on the Sabbath, coupled with the establishment of a Sabbath-keeping line of boats on the canal, and a pioneer line of coaches on the road. These all had their origin in the heart of that man of christian earnestness and energy, Josiah Bissell, Jr., first elder of this church.

On the 28th of February, 1827, a formal organization was perfected by the enrollment of nineteen persons with letters from the First and Brick Presbyterian churches. Messrs. Salmon Scofield and Josiah Bissell, Jr., were elected elders — both long deceased, as are all the other founders.

This temporary but honored place of worship ere long yielded to one more commodious, substantial and attractive, on the corner of Main and North Clinton streets. But in so doing a debt was contracted which resulted in the selling of the property to the Second Baptist society at a nominal amount of $7000. The first pastor, Rev. (now Dr.) Joel Parker, having accepted a call to New York city, Rev. Charles G. Finney preached for six months, beginning early in September, 1830, with abundant results in addition to membership and strength. In May, 1831, Rev. Luke Lyons was called to the pastorate, but remained a short time, when he and a large number withdrew and organized a Free Church on the corner of Court and Stone streets. After the dismission of Mr. Lyons, Rev. Mr. (now Dr.) W. C. Wisner, of Lockport, was called to the pastorate, but left after a brief service. Then came a period of depression threatening the very life of the organization. A few remained firm and hopeful. These held occasional service in the old Methodist church on St. Paul street, south of the present theatre, and in the Scotch church on the corner of Stillson and Main streets, waiting the indication of the Divine will. It was in the year 1834 that Rev. William Mack, then on his way to Canada, accepted an invitation to pass a few Sabbaths here, which resulted in his assuming the pastorate, the place of worship being the upper room of the old High

School house, which then stood on the site now occupied by the present imposing church edifice. For five years (February, 1835, to June, 1839), Mr. Mack ministered with much ability and usefulness, when he resigned, and now resides in Columbia, Tennessee. The congregation then erected a small stone structure on the south side of Main street, which was subsequently enlarged and beautified, but was finally destroyed by fire in the autumn of 1858. On the first Sabbath of February, 1840, Rev. (now Dr.) Albert G. Hall commenced his labors, which have extended to the present time, and during whose ministry about nine hundred have been added to the church, one-half or more upon profession of their faith. The Sabbath school has been a nursery indeed, fifteen preachers of the Gospel having gone from it, through the church, into the ministry, twelve of whom are now living and three are deceased; one was a foreign missionary.

The present edifice, after plans by Upjohn, of New York, was erected in the year 1859, at an expense of about $38,000. The nineteen persons constituting the membership in 1826 have arisen to four hundred, with two hundred and fifty in the Sabbath school, and other elements indicating prosperity. In his "Twenty-fifth Anniversary Sermon," delivered January 29, 1865, the pastor speaks of losses by death of such persons as Messrs. Josiah Bissell, Jr., George A. Hollister, Selah Matthews, a model elder, "Father" Albee. J. W. Smith, M.D., "the beloved physician"; Abijah Gould, Platt Starr, father of Hon. Frederick Starr; David Scoville, "Father" Eli Stillson, Asahel Fitch, Joseph Combs, Dr. Moses Long, U. G. Squier, Munn Morgan, John S.

Allen, James Hair, Alvin S. French, Virgil Chittenden, William Cogswell, John C. Merrill, George Clark, Deacon Isaac Hobbie, Mr. Crittenden, Mr. Granger, Anson House, Rev. Charles Ray, for many years a missionary in India, and father of Rev. Charles Ray of Wyoming; Hon. W. C. Bloss, with many wives, mothers and sisters, who, having finished the work given them to do have ascended to their heavenly home. "Their works do follow them, and their memory is blessed."

This church has recently sustained no ordinary loss in the death of Mr. Emmet H. Hollister, son of one of the founders.

PASTORS.

Rev. Joel Parker, D.D., was born in Bethel, Vt., in 1799; studied at Hamilton college and Auburn seminary; accepted a call as first pastor of the Third church of Rochester, upon a salary of "a half of brother Josiah Bissell's biscuit, as long as he had one," or more financially expressed, $130 for the first six months, and $800 per annum afterwards. After a two years' pastorate, he was induced, after much solicitation, to remove to New York and commence a new enterprise in that city. Having labored there with great energy and success for four years, he went to New Orleans as pastor of the First Presbyterian church of that southern metropolis, but returned to New York and assumed charge of the Broadway Tabernacle in 1838, during which time he acted as president of the Union Theological seminary, then recently established. In 1842 he removed to Philadelphia, Pa., as pastor of the Clinton street church, and back to New York, as successor of the Rev. Dr. Erskine Mason, on Bleecker street, in 1842. The year 1862 found him pastor of the Park street church of Newark, which ill health compelled him to resign, but in which city he now resides. Few ministers of Christ spent thirty-five years of more abundant labor and ample success and large repute than did Dr. Parker between 1827 and 1862. He will long live in the esteem and gratitude of many hearts.

Rev. Luke Lyons came to the "village" from Courtland, in 1831, remaining for a few months in charge of the Third, and then of a new organization on Court street, till about 1845, when he went to Illinois, and died.

Rev. William Mack, D.D., came to this city from the seminary at Princeton; served the church with ability for two years, and went south, where he now resides, in Columbia, Tenn.

Rev. William Carpenter Wisner, D.D., is a native of Elmira, N. Y., and a graduate of Union college. He studied theology with his father, William Wisner, D.D., for many years pastor of the Presbyterian church at Ithaca, and for a time of the Brick church of this city. He took charge of the Third church in 1832, but resigned in two years, on account of ill health, and has since ministered to the First church of Lockport. It was during Dr. Wisner's pastorate here that the cholera prevailed in the city with such sad results. The illness of Drs. Penny and Wisner, Sr., threw upon the young pastor an amount of labor and care beyond the endurance of one not of sturdiest frame. Dr. Wisner often preaches in the city, and always with acceptance and usefulness.

Rev. Albert Gallatin Hall, D.D., was born in Whitehall, Washington county, N. Y.; after coming to this city, became a member of the Third Presbyterian church; pursued his classical studies principally in private, with a brief term at the collegiate institution, and his theological at home after his day's labor as printer and editor of a weekly journal, in support of his family; was licensed to preach July 1, 1835; ministered to a church in Penfield, N. Y.; became pastor of the Third in February, 1840, which position he still holds with rare ability, universal esteem, and powerful influence for good in his parish and region. A character formed under circumstances like those referred to must be of a nature to make itself felt. Dr. Hall is no ordinary man in thought and power.

S. S. SUPERINTENDENTS.

The superintendents of the Sabbath school have been, Josiah Bissell, Jr., Salmon Scofield, Albert G. Hall (now pastor), Joseph B. Bloss, Samuel W. Lee, Selah Matthews, Jonathan Copeland (now Rev.), John G. Parker, William Shepherd, C. C. Colt, George A. Hollister, Joseph D. Husbands, John Graves, Ira Belden, Charles Ray (now Rev.) William T. Cushing, William J. Armitage, Emmet H. Hollister, Jesse Shepherd, David H. Little, and Manly D. Rowley.

MEMBERS OF THIS CHURCH WHO HAVE ENTERED THE MINISTRY.

Rev. Albert G. Hall, D.D., now in the thirty-first year of his pastorate.
Rev. Hezekiah Pierrepont, in Rochester.
Rev. Richard DeForest, in Rochester
Rev. T. Reaves Chipman, deceased.
Rev. Samuel M. Bayliss, Darlington, Md.
Rev. Jonathan Copeland.
Rev. Charles Ray, Wyoming, N. Y.
Rev. Gavin Longmuir.
Rev. Charles W. Wood, Oakfield, N. Y.

SUMMARY, JULY 1, 1871.

Pastor—Rev. Albert G. Hall, D.D.

Elders—Messrs. Nathaniel Hayward, William Shepherd, Thomas B. Husbands, Ira Cook, John Voorhees, Joseph Harris, William F. Cogswell.

Deacons—Messrs. James Young, Storrs Hayward, John Evershed.

Trustees—W. J. Armitage, Edward Harris, W. G. Watson, D. P. Allen, B. P. Robinson, M. D. Rowley, A. Reynolds, J. G. Luitwiler, Peter Schenck.

S. S. Superintendent—M. D. Rowley.

S. S. Scholars—250.

Communicants—400.

CENTRAL CHURCH.

In March, 1836, several members of the First Presbyterian church met to discuss the expediency of establishing another evangelical church within the limits of the city. After much prayer and consultation, it was unanimously resolved, "That the present circumstances of Rochester call for the establishment of another church within its limits."

The distinguishing characteristics of this new enterprise were declared to be: 1st. It was to be a missionary church, established upon principles of high christian consecration and devotedness. 2d. A free church, embracing a Bethel interest. 3d. Open for free discussion on all subjects of morals, etc., such as temperance, slavery, etc. 4th. Its secular as well as its religious affairs to be in the hands of the church exclusively.

In August, 1836, thirty-nine persons, members of the First church, were organized by the Presbytery of Rochester, under the name of the "Bethel Presbyterian church of Rochester." Their names were Michael B. Bateham, Preston, Eunice, Henry F., William P. and Elvira N. Smith, Joseph Farley, Theodore B. and Julia M. Hamilton, Joseph, Nancy and Newell A.

Stone, Mary Jane Porter, Thomas Adams, William S. Bishop, George A. and Frances Avery, Richard P. and Mary P. Wilkins, Spencer Davis, Ebenezer and Polly Knapp, Appollos Luce, Aurelia S. Adams, Mary M. Cook, Eliza Davis, John F. Bush, John Biden, Jr., Walter S., Henry D. and Elizabeth S. Griffith, William and Lydia Cook, Josiah and Mary Newell, John and Louisa Stitt, Lydia and Fanny E. Hatch. Of these original thirty-nine founders, fifteen are still living, seven are residents of the city, and and three are in communion with the church, viz: Henry F. and Elvira N. Smith and Joseph Stone. The first bench of elders were Messrs. George A. Avery (deceased), Walter S. Griffith (of Brooklyn), and Preston Smith (deceased).

A substantial stone edifice was erected, during the fall and winter, on Washington street, adjacent to the Erie canal, costing $15,000.

The Rev. George S. Boardman was installed as first pastor October 19, 1837, and resigned July, 1842. His pastoral and Sabbath school labors were so greatly blessed of God that the little band became two hundred and fifty strong. In February, 1842, Rev. Charles G. Finney, of Oberlin, Ohio, assisted the pastor in a series of meetings, which resulted in the hopeful conversion of three hundred and fifty persons, many of whom ranked as our most influention citizens. These united with the following churches: St. Luke's, Episcopal, 75; First Presbyterian, 24; Brick, Presbyterian, 89; Third Presbyterian, 20; Washington street, Presbyterian, 16; First Baptist, 12; Methodist, two churches, 115.

In 1841 the name of the church was changed from Bethel Free church to that of the Washington street church.

In March, 1843, the church withdrew from the Presbytery and became independent, so continuing till 1844, when it resumed its former ecclesiastical position.

Between July, 1842, and February, 1845, the church being without a pastor, the pulpit was supplied by Rev. John T. Avery, Rev. Bassett, Rev. G. H. R. Shumway, Rev. Fred. W. Graves, and Rev. Parsons C. Hastings. This was a period of declension, and the membership sank to two hundred and three members, of whom fifty were non-residents.

During August, 1844, a colony, consisting of ten heads of families with their households, responded to the Macedonian cry, and with noble generosity left the Brick church to join this; thus adding greatly to our working material, especially in the Sabbath school.

The Rev. Milo J. Hickok, D.D., was installed as second pastor, February 25, 1845, resigning March 15, 1854. These were years of growth and general prosperity. The early missionary spirit was revived and much strengthened by an admirable course of addresses delivered by the pastor, assisted by maps, some of which were prepared by his own hands. This had much to do with sending two female missionaries to foreign lands.

Rev. Frank F. Ellinwood, D.D., was installed as third pastor January 9, 1855, resigning January 24, 1866, much to the regret of the people, who voted him $100 per month for a year. Ill health was the sole but imperative cause.

The congregation continued to worship on Washington street till the completion of their new and commodious edifice on Sophia street, which was dedicated April 8, 1858. This was a marked event in the history of the church, not only on account of the change of name from Washington street church to Central Presbyterian church, but more by the evident blessing of God, in things temporal and spiritual, from year to year. Several revivals occurred, the most abundant in results being under the labors of Rev. E. P. Hammond, when large accessions were made, especially from the youth.

Rev. Samuel M. Campbell, D.D., the fourth pastor and present incumbent, was installed June 14, 1866.

A vigorous mission Sabbath school, planted and sustained by this church for more than ten years, on West avenue, was, on the 11th of April, 1868, set off as a separate organization, under the title of the Westminster church of Rochester, with eighty-two members, all of whom were from the parent body.

In the year 1869 another mission school was established on Lake avenue, which has now about two hundred scholars, with a hopeful future, under the efficient superintendence of Mr. William A. Hubbard, an elder of the church, aided by a corps of teachers of great earnestness and devotion.

PASTORS.

Rev. George Smith Boardman, D.D., is a native of Albany, N. Y., and a graduate of Union college and of Princeton seminary. Having spent sixteen years as pastor of the First church in Watertown, N.Y., he removed to Rochester in 1837, and became pastor of the Central till 1842, when he resigned and assumed a pastorate at Cherry Valley, and then at Cazenovia. Ill health has required a relinquishment of a pastorate, though still preaching with frequency, supplying the church at Ogdensburgh during the absence in Europe of their pastor, Dr. L. M. Miller.

Rev. Milo Judson Hickok, D.D., was born at New Haven, Vt.; graduated at Middlebury college and Union seminary, N. Y.; came to Rochester in 1845, where he labored with great energy for nine years, and then went to Scranton, Pa., where he was pastor for fourteen years, when a stroke of paralysis disabled him for further public work, and he is spending his last days at Marietta, Ohio.

Rev. Frank Field Ellinwood, D.D., was born in Clinton, N. Y.; studied at Hamilton college and at both Auburn and Princeton seminaries; was settled at Belvidere, N. Y., from whence he came to Rochester in November, 1854, where he remained till 1865, when ill health compelled him to leave a devoted people, among whom he had labored with great acceptance and success for eleven years. Returning from a long tour abroad, he assumed the secretaryship of the Church Erection committee, which he held till the re-union. He had charge of the $5,000,000 memorial fund, upon completing which he became co-secretary of the Board of Foreign Missions, having declined a professorship in the Theological seminary at Pittsburgh, to which he had been elected.

Rev. Samuel M. Campbell, D.D., was born in Campbelltown, Steuben county, N. Y.; pursued his classical studies privately, and his theological at Auburn. His first ministerial charge was at Parr's Hill; his second (a year), at Dansville; his third, at Utica (Westminster), from whence he came to Rochester, March 1, 1866.

ELDERS.

George A. Avery, Walter S. Griffith, Preston Smith (deceased), ordained 1836; Philip Thurber, 1838; Calvin H. Hamilton (deceased), William S. Bishop (deceased), 1841; Charles Freeman (deceased), 1844; William Alling, Lyman Cook, 1845; John G. Dabney (deceased), Solon C. Avery (deceased), Orlando Hastings (deceased), 1848; Frederick Starr (deceased), 1845; John N. Harder, 1856; Steuben S. Forbes, 1865; Elias Child, George W. Parsons, Henry Churchill, 1860; Frederick W. Dewey, William A. Hubbard, David A. Baldwin, M.D., and Lewis A. Alling, 1865.

Whole number of persons admitted to this church since its formation in 1836, 1775; of this number, 811 were upon profession of their faith (631 from the Sabbath school), and 964 by letter.

MINISTERS AND MISSIONARIES FROM THIS CHURCH.

Rev. C. W. Torrey.
Rev. Frederick J. Jackson, at Tarrytown, N. Y.
Rev. Dillis D. Hamilton, at Pompeii, Mich.
Rev. George S. Bishop, at Newburgh, N. Y.
Rev. Willis C. Gaylord, at Ossian, N. Y.

Miss Fanny M. Nelson (Mrs. S. McKinney), South Africa.

Miss Isabella J. Atwater (Mrs. M. White), China.

Miss Hattie Seymor, East Turkey.

Miss Carrie E. Bush (daughter of Rev. Charles P. Bush, D.D.), East Turkey.

SABBATH SCHOOL.

The Bethel Sabbath school of the city of Rochester was organized August 12, 1836, the first session being in the Crane school house, on the north side of Buffalo street, between Sophia and Washington streets. Present at the organization, Messrs. W. S. Griffith, William Cook, William S. Bishop, John Stitt, Josiah Newell, Preston Smith, Theodore B. Hamilton, Joseph Farley, John F. Bush, John Biden, Jr., Richard P. Wilkins, and M. B. Bateham, with Mrs. William Cook, T. B. Hamilton, Joseph Stone, and Misses Frances Hatch and Naomi Davis — in all eighteen. Of these there are now living, Messrs. Griffith, Bateham, Farley, Bush, and H. A. Brewster. Of the twenty-six scholars present at the first session, two are now connected with the school, viz: Mr. Henry F. Smith, secretary and treasurer, and his sister, Mrs. Elvira Smith Allen, a teacher.

The superintendents have been, W. S. Griffith, 1836-9; William S. Bishop, 1839-42; George W. Parsons, 1842 to 1871, less one year on account of sickness, and who is now in his twenty-eighth year of service.

Average attendance of scholars during thirty-four

years, 253; average attendance of teachers during thirty-four years, 42. Added to the church, of scholars, during thirty-four years, 631. Enlistments during the late war, from the Sabbath school, 110—of whom fifteen are known to have died on the field or in the hospital. The missionaries before named were teachers in the Sabbath school.

The Young People's Missionary Society, organized in 1846, and lately re-organized, is doing a noble work in city, home, and foreign missions. Contributions to various benevolent objects have come largely from the Sabbath school.

BENEVOLENCE.

The first decade was a season of planting, of church building, etc.; hence the amounts paid to outside objects were small.

First Decade.

From August 1, 1836, to January 1, 1847:

Foreign missions,	$378 73	
Home "	411 76	
Miscellaneous objects,	692 10	
		$1,482 59

Second Decade.

January 1, 1847, to January 1, 1857:

Foreign missions,	$2,767 64	
Home "	1,841 82	
Miscellaneous objects,	4,486 54	
		$9,096 00

Third Decade.

January 1, 1857, to January 1, 1867:

Foreign missions,	$8,342 91	
Home "	4,572 56	
Miscellaneous objects,	29,239 40	
		$42,154 87

Fourth Decade (one-half).

January 1, 1867, to January 1, 1871:

Foreign missions,	$4,938 50	
Home "	8336 84	
Miscellaneous objects,	11,600 10	
		$24,875 44

New place of worship in 1858, $41,000, less
  by $8,600, avails of the old, $32,400
Missions chapel in 1860-1,   3,000
Organ,   5,000

SUMMARY, JULY 1, 1871.

Pastor—Rev. Samuel S. Campbell, D.D.

Elders—Messrs. William Alling, John N. Harder, Steuben S. Forbes, George W. Parsons, Henry Churchill, Frederick W. Dewey, William A. Hubbard, Lewis H. Alling.

Trustees—Messrs. George W. Parsons, William A. Hubbard, H. Austin Brewster, Lewis H. Alling, William S. Alling, Herbert Churchill, Henry F. Smith, A. M. Hastings, and Samuel Sloan.

S. S. Superintendent—George W. Parsons.

No. of Scholars—775.

Church Communicants—700.

CALVARY CHURCH.

Early in the year 1847, Rev. Richard DeForest purchased a lot in the south-east part of the city, on which he erected a small building, containing one room, and then went through the neighborhood informing the residents that a Sabbath school would be commenced on the next Lord's day morning, followed by preaching in the afternoon. Forty scholars were present at the former service, and a crowd at the latter. This occurred on the 12th of December, 1847. Special religious interest was soon manifest, which resulted in a considerable ingathering of converts, thus preparing the way for a formal ecclesiastical organization on the 26th of March, 1848, under the name of the St. Paul street Congregational church. The sermon was preached by Rev. Henry E. Peck, pastor of the State street Congregational church, and twenty-six persons enrolled themselves as members in full communion. In the May following a church edifice was begun on the corner of South avenue and Jefferson street, which, after months of effort made by Mr. DeForest in obtaining funds, was completed and dedicated to the worship of God, November 3, 1850; the sermon being preached by President Mahan, of Oberlin, Ohio.

The ecclesiastical relations and forms of worship were Congregational, and so continued until another church of the same denomination, and other causes, so affected the finances that a sale of the property became imperative. It was purchased by L. A. Ward, Esq., with a view of its becoming Presbyterian, which has been the case ever since.

The Presbytery of Rochester city (old school), at their stated spring meeting in 1856, appointed a committee, consisting of Revs. A. G. Hall, D.D., J. H. McIlvaine, D.D., R. H. Richardson, and James Harkness, and Elders L. A. Ward, W. T. Cushing, and Benton. This committee met on the 15th day of June, 1856, in what was known as South St. Paul street Congregational church, where, with others, the following persons were assembled, and presented to the committee letters of membership and dismission from their respective churches, with the view of being constituted into a new church, namely:

From the Third Presbyterian church—William Stebbins, Eliza B. Stebbins, William T. Cushing, Arabella Cushing, Olive Howes, Helen M. Howes, J. G. Stothoff, Henrietta Dempsey, Hannah Ray, Mercy Ingraham.

From the St. Paul street Congregational church—Elizabeth Blum, Eliza Barrett, James Barton, Charles Barton, James G. Badger, Catharine Badger.

These sixteen persons were in the usual way constituted into a new and independent ecclesiastical organization, to be named and known as the Calvary Presbyterian church of Rochester.

At the same time William Stebbins and William T.

Cushing were elected and installed ruling elders in the infant church.

Few in number and feeble in resources, this little company, like the crew of a little boat launched upon the open sea, embarked with fear and trembling upon their new career. They had not assembled, however, many weeks, when they resolved to call and settle over them a pastor of their own. Accordingly on the 30th of July of the same year, they extended a call to Rev. Charles Ray, which was accepted. Mr. Ray entered the field with zeal and energy, and continued his pastoral labors among them until August 15th, 1858, when a variety of circumstances concurred to decide him that it was his duty to resign and leave.

Though now considerably increased in numbers, yet many were the discouragements and difficulties which visited this little church at this time. The pulpit, however, continued to be supplied by Rev. F. DeW. Ward, D.D., of Geneseo, Rev. J. Nichols, Rev. W. Howell Taylor, and others, till in April, 1860, they again rallied and united in calling for their pastor Rev. Bellville Roberts. Mr. Roberts manfully faced the difficulties before him. During his ministry many were added to the church, and through his untiring efforts the entire debt on the house of worship was wiped off. Still the society was pecuniarily weak, and it was found difficult to meet the necessary expenses, notwithstanding that a certain amount of aid was obtained from the B. of D. M. Owing to this and to the declining health of his wife, Mr. Roberts resolved to resign and remove west, which he did after a pastorate of some four years.

Once more the little flock found themselves without a shepherd; but Providence did not forsake them. Their minds ere long were directed to Rev. Alfred Yeomans, who was earnestly invited to come and take the oversight of them. He consented; and from his amiable character, intellectual ability, and particularly from his relationship to Dr. Yeomans, pastor of the St. Peter's church, being his brother, great hopes were entertained for Calvary; the day of its deliverance from toil and peril and privations of its pilgrimage through the wilderness was deemed near at hand. Mr. Yeomans, however, much to their grief, continued among them but for one brief year, and even during that brief period his labors were sadly interrupted once and again by ill health. He left in the fall of 1866.

While passing through these repeated changes and trials, this congregation was much burdened and harassed by city taxation. Situated upon a corner, it had been subject to double charges for gradings, sewers and sidewalks, which brought in a series of heavy bills, and the end of this is not yet. What would have been in this way a light matter to an old and strong church society, was found and felt here to be a burden heavy to be borne. To meet these onerous obligations, many have been the sacrifices silently and cheerfully made, which are worthy to be reckoned with the widow's offering, that drew forth the Saviour's high commendation.

After Rev. Mr. Yeomans' departure, the desk was supplied by different individuals for several months, till in the following winter the society once more united in a call to Rev. H. W. Morris, which he accepted, but did not regularly enter upon his pastoral duties until March 17, 1867. Mr. Morris remains the pastor to the present day, and by the blessing of God upon his pulpit and pastoral labors, the church has made, though not rapid, yet steady progress. In the winter of 1869 a very precious visitation of grace was enjoyed, there being among those received at one communion ten heads of families. During his ministry, as the sessional records exhibit, the membership has been nearly doubled, the general congregation much increased and established in its character, so that the church to-day occupies a position in the public estimation far in advance of what it ever did before. The corner-stone of a reconstructed church has lately been laid.

PASTORS.

Rev. Richard DeForest, a native of New York city, is of French descent, his ancestor two centuries back being a refugee to New Amsterdam (now New York). After a course of classical and theological instruction under Prof. F. N. Benedict, and at Auburn seminary, Mr. DeForest labored as an evangelist in this State and at the west till he returned and was first pastor of St. Paul street Congregational church. He now resides in the city.

Rev. Charles Ray, son of Rev. Edward and Sarah Ray, was born at Calcutta, India, in 1829; accompanied his parents to this country in 1839; became a member of the Third Presbyterian church (Dr. A. G. Hall, pastor); pursued his education at Union college and Princeton Theological seminary; held ministerial charges at Piffard, Seneca Falls, Calvary church, Rochester, was Principal of Geneseo academy, and was pastor of a church in the pleasant village of Wyoming, which he recently left on account of ill health, having served with eminent ability and usefulness.

Rev. Bellville Roberts spent four years of earnest effort in the pastorate of this church, witnessing many results of his ministry, and then removed to Wheeling, Va., where he now resides. He was an able and faithful preacher.

Rev. Alfred Yeomans, a native of N. Adams, Mass., and son of Rev. Dr. John W. Yeomans, moderator of general assembly in 1860, was educated at Princeton college and seminary; ministered to churches at New Hampton, N. J., Rochester (Calvary), Bellefonte, Penn., and now at Orange, N. J., as successor of his brother, Rev. E. D. Yeomans, D.D., formerly of St. Peter's. Ill health compelled these frequent changes, always to the regret of the people whom he ably and usefully served.

Rev. Henry W. Morris is a native of Wales; was educated in England, and has passed his ministerial life in America. His first pastorate was a Presbyterian church at Martinburgh, Lewis county, N. Y.; his second at Little Falls. He took charge of Calvary church in 1867, where he is meeting his duties with great satisfaction in a section of the city demanding much labor and patience.

SUMMARY, JULY 1, 1871.

Pastor—Rev. Henry W. Morris.

Elders—Messrs. William Stebbins, David L. Hunn, and F. S. Stebbins.

Deacons—None.

Trustees—Messrs. F. S. Stebbins, Thomas S. Oliver, Judson Knickerbocker, D. L. Hunn, and C. B. Corser.

S. S. Superintendent—J. R. Reeves.

S. S. Pupils—70.

Total Membership—118.

SAINT PETER'S CHURCH.

In May, 1852, a well known citizen of Rochester, then a member of the First Presbyterian church, commenced the construction of a new church edifice upon a lot of land owned by him on Grove street. The location was central to a large American population with no place of worship. His desire was to supply this imperative demand by the organization of a new Presbyterian church, and with an order of worship which should more fully develop the united devotion of the whole congregation than is now customary in churches of that denomination.

On the 7th of June, 1852, the corner-stone of Saint Peter's was laid by Rev. J. H. McIlvaine, D.D., of the First church, with an appropriate address; other parts of the service being taken by Rev. Messrs. Hill and Ward of the Presbyterian, Rev. W. H. Goodwin, D.D., of the Methodist Episcopal, Rev. Mr. Howard of the Baptist, and Rev. Dr. Chester Dewey of the Congregational churches. The edifice was completed at an expense of $35,000, and dedicated on the 25th of October, 1853; the sermon being preached by Rev. Dr. McIlvaine, and other parts conducted by Rev. A. G. Hall, D.D., Rev. F. DeW. Ward, D.D., of Genesco, and other clergymen. The first Sabbath service was held October 3, 1853, the sermon being preached by Rev. Dr. Huntington, then of Albany and now of Auburn Theological seminary.

The order of public service then adopted, and maintained to the present time, with slight changes, is as follows:

1. Salutation and doxology.
2. Profession of faith, in the use of the Apostles' Creed, by minister and people.
3. Invocation, and the Lord's Prayer, the people joining in the latter.
4. Reading the Ten Commandments, with a response by the choir.
5. Invitation, and confession of sin.
6. Hymn.
7. Reading the Scriptures.
8. Anthem.
9. Reading Psalter by minister and people responsively.
10. Hymn.
11. General prayer.
12. Anthem.
13. Sermon.
14. Closing prayer (brief).
15. Doxology.
16. Benediction.

The above is the order of morning service; the evening service is slightly different, as also on special occasions. A Book of Worship is used by minister and congregation, containing the order of service, both general and special; the chants and anthems being generally sung by the choir, and hymns by the choir and people. The officiating minister wears the ordinary black gown and the bands in conducting all the services. No form of prayer is used except the Lord's Prayer.

A record has been kept of every Sabbath service since the opening of the house, which contains the names of two hundred and forty-nine clergymen, of whom eleven were ex-Moderators of the Presbyterian General Assemblys.

On the 13th of December, 1853, a special meeting of the Presbytery of Rochester city (old school) was held at the chapel of Saint Peter's, at which the following persons presented certificates of dismission from the various churches mentioned, and were constituted by Presbytery "The Saint Peter's Presbyterian church of the city of Rochester."

Levi A., Harriet, Mary E. and William H. Ward, Lorenzo D. and Caroline C. Ely, Lowell and Chloe Bullen, Mrs. Susan W. Selden, Miss Ellen M. Kemp, Miss Jane Bradbury, and Mrs. Emily Chumasero, from the First Presbyterian church of Rochester; Dr. John F. and Elizabeth A. Whitbeck, from the Brick church; Edward A. and Eugenie C. Raymond, Samuel B. and Harriet M. Raymond, Mrs. Caroline E. McAlpine, and Mrs. Caroline B. Dwinelle, from the Third church; James, Mrs. Resinah and Miss Ann E. Murray, from Washington street church; Mrs. Betsey L. Oothout, from the Presbyterian church at Holley, N. Y.; Mrs. Emily R. Beckwith, from Saint John's Methodist Episcopal church, Rochester; Mrs.

Mary Ann Holyland, from Free Baptist church, Rochester; John S. and Chloe Dean, from Congregational church, Armsville.

Of the twenty-eight founders of Saint Peter's, eleven are still members of this church. At this first meeting an election of officers was held, which resulted in the unanimous choice of Messrs. L. A. Ward and Edward A. Raymond as elders, their ordination taking place on the first Sabbath of January, 1854; Rev. A. G. Hall, D.D., by appointment of Presbytery, conducting the services, which were preceded by a sermon from Rev. Dr. McIlvaine.

Edward A. Raymond was chosen clerk and treasurer of session on the 12th of December, 1853, and has so continued to the present time, with the exception of three years, when he was absent from the city.

PASTORS AND STATED SUPPLIES.

Rev. John T. Coit was stated supply from September 3, 1854, to January 7, 1855.

Rev. Leonard W. Bacon was stated supply from March 25, 1855, to September 16, 1855.

Rev. Richard H. Richardson was installed first pastor June 10, 1856 (sermon by Rev. Dr. Hall), and resigned November 30, 1857.

Rev. Everard Kempshall was stated supply from December 23, 1857, to May 16, 1858.

Rev. Joseph H. Towne, D.D., was installed second pastor October 28, 1858 (sermon by Rev. Dr. McIlvaine), and resigned March 9, 1860.

Rev. John T. Coit was installed as third pastor

(sermon by Rev. William James, D.D., of Albany) June 3, 1860, and died at Albion January 23, 1863.

Rev. E. D. Yeomans, D.D., was installed fourth pastor June 7, 1863 (sermon by Rev. Dr. Hall), and resigned, on account of failing health, April 28, 1867. He died at Orange, N. J., August, 1869.

Rev. James M. Crowell, D.D., was installed fifth pastor May 16, 1869 (sermon by Rev. Dr. Hall), and resigned December 6, 1870.

The church is now without a pastor.

ELDERS.

Messrs. Levi A. Ward and Edward A. Raymond were elected at the organization of the church, and are still in office. Messrs. William Slocomb and Hiram Banker were elected November 10, 1858. The former, now in his ninetieth year, is too much of an invalid to leave his home; the latter died September 22, 1864. Mr. Jerome B. Stillson was ordained and installed August 3, 1860; and Mr. David A. Mitchell April 24, 1864, and died June 22, 1866. Messrs. Jonathan E. Pierpont and Marcus K. Woodbury were ordained and installed July 24, 1870.

DEACONS.

Messrs. Joseph B. Ward and Marcus K. Woodbury were ordained and installed March 13, 1869. Mr. Woodbury having been elected a ruling elder, the active duties of the office are performed by Mr. Ward.

TRUSTEES.

The first elected were Messrs. Samuel L. Selden, Josiah W. Bissell, Charles H. Clark, B. R. McAlpine, Lorenzo D. Ely, Samuel B. Raymond, Jerome B. Stillson, Charles A. Jones, and Charles F. Smith. Subsequently there were elected Messrs. John W. Dwinelle, Hubbard S. Allis, M. K. Woodbury, George P. Townsend, Joseph B. Ward, Wallace Darrow, Simeon L. Brewster, L. Ward Clarke, P. B. Veile, J. E. Pierpont, and W. S. Kimball.

SABBATH SCHOOL.

Was organized December, 1853, with forty-one scholars. The superintendents have been Messrs. E. A. Raymond, until 1857; L. A. Ward, until 1860; Joseph B. Ward, until 1865; Rev. Dr. Yeomans, pastor, a few months; J. E. Pierpont, until 1866; E. N. Hoyt, until 1868; when Mr. John W. Stebbins was chosen, and is now in office. The Sabbath school has regularly and largely contributed to the benevolent operations of the church.

George Kemp Ward, a member of this Sabbath school and church, is now pursuing his theological studies at Princeton.

CHURCH EDIFICE.

A deed of the church property was executed and delivered to the trustees by the founder March 27, 1867. The first edifice was destroyed by fire March

18, 1868, but was immediately rebuilt at an expense of about $49,000. During the interim services were held in Christ's church chapel (Episcopal) and Second Baptist church, the use of which churches had been tendered in a spirit of christian generosity which was gratefully appreciated by the afflicted parish. Worship was resumed in the reconstructed chapel January 24, 1869, and in the main audience room June 6, 1869.

PASTORS.

Rev. Richard H. Richardson, D.D., is a native of Lexington, Ky., and graduate of Princeton college and Theological seminary; was pastor of the North Presbyterian church of Chicago, which he left to assume charge of Saint Peter's, and after a pastorate of one and a half years, resigned and removed to Redbank, Putnam county, N. Y., then to Newburyport, Mass., and thence to Trenton, N. J., where he now resides, as pastor of the Fourth Presbyterian church. A gentleman of scholarship and pulpit power, his ministrations have been eminently successful in the several places of his abode and public services.

Rev. Joseph H. Towne, D.D., came to this city from Chicago; presided over Saint Peter's for two years, and left for Milwaukee, and then for Buffalo. His lectures on "Pilgrim's Progress" will be long remembered in this parish and in the city.

Rev. John Townsend Coit, son of George and Hannah T. Coit, was a native of Buffalo, N. Y.; a graduate of Yale college and Andover Theological seminary. Returning from Germany, where he pursued his studies for one and a half years at Gottingen and Halle, under Professor Tholuck and gifted associates, he accepted a call to the Presbyterian church at Albion, which position he held for five years, commencing his ministry as third pastor of Saint Peter's June 1, 1860. He was no stranger to the people here, having acted as stated supply, after returning from Europe. Three years passed away with entire satisfaction and much profit to his increasingly attached parishioners, when upon a visit to his friends at Albion he was suddenly called to a higher sphere of labor and purer worship above. When told that he could live but a short time, he said, "Doctor, you surprise me; I never dreamed of this; but I can say with truth that I am ready, nay, joyous, to go." After some moments of rest, he asked, as in surprise, "Can this be death? Then how beautiful it is to die! I already see the coming glories! This is paradise! Death has no appalling features." "Doctor," said he, "is it not strange that when dying as I know my body is, my mind should apprehend these things so clearly?" Well might by-standers exclaim,

"Is that a death-bed where a christian lies?"
"Yes, but not his; 't is death itself there dies."

A tablet of Nova Scotia stone, placed on the right of the pulpit, reads thus:

"John Townsend Coit.
Died Jan'y 23, 1863, in the 39th year of his age, and the third of his pastorate of this church. His life of faithful devotion to his work, made beautiful by a character of rare purity and symmetry, was crowned by a death of triumphant hope."

Rev. Edward Dorr Yeomans, D.D., son of the late Dr. J. W. Yeomans (moderator of general assembly in 1860), was born at North Adams, Mass.; pursued his classical studies at Easton, Pa., and his theological at Princeton; was licensed to preach at the early age of seventeen and a half years; became minister of churches in Warren Run, Penn., Fourth Presbyterian of Trenton, N. J., and in May, 1863, assumed the pastorate of St. Peter's, in this city, which position he held with marked ability until his removal to Orange, N. J. Here he labored with whatever strength was given him, till August 23d, when he died of apoplexy. The immediate cause of his early and lamented death was overtasking his brain in sermon writing and translation of Lange's Commentary on John, with similar and unremitting exertion of his mental powers and nervous energy. As a strong thinker, a close student, and an accomplished scholar, Dr. Yeomans has had few equals.

A beautiful tablet, in bronze — the Christmas gift of a parishioner — has been placed on the inner wall of the church on the left of the pulpit, with the following inscription engraved upon it in illuminated letters:

"Edward Dorr Yeomans, D.D.
Pastor MDCCCLXIII–LXVII.
Learned in the Scriptures and the Fathers; eloquent and faithful in his ministry; he finished his work at noon-day and went to his rest August XXVII, MDCCCLXVIII — Aged XXXIX years."

James M. Crowell, D.D., was born in Philadelphia; made a profession of religion at the age of fourteen, under the ministry of his cousin, Rev. John Crowell, D.D., now of Odessa, Del.; graduated at Princeton college (of which he is now a trustee) and seminary; has ministered at Octarara, Penn., and the Seventh Presbyterian church of Philadelphia, and removed to Rochester as pastor of Saint Peter's from May 5, 1869, to December, 1870, when he returned to his native city to enter upon a new enterprise — the Woodland church, where he now resides. Laborious, earnest, fervent and practical, his ministry has been and is likely to continue successful in leading sinners to the Saviour and saints to higher attainments of holiness.

SUMMARY, JULY 1, 1871.

Pastor—

Elders—Messrs. L. A. Ward, Edward A. Raymond, William Slocomb, Jonathan E. Pierpont, and Marcus K. Woodbury.

Deacon—Mr. Joseph B. Ward.

S. S. Superintendents—Mr. John W. Stebbins and Mrs. John C. Chumasero.

Number of Scholars—383.

Number of Church Communicants—248.

Trustees—Messrs. Lorenzo D. Ely, Freeman Clarke, John C. Chumasero, Daniel Lowry, Theodore Bacon, W. H. Ward, D. P. Westcott, F. B. Mitchell, and Abraham Bebee.

WESTMINSTER CHURCH.

On the 29th of June, 1856, a Sunday school was organized in a building at the corner of West avenue and Prospect streets. It was sustained as a Mission school by the Central Presbyterian church, then under the pastorate of Rev. F. F. Ellinwood, D.D., and was under the care of the late William S. Bishop, Esq.

About the same time, another Sunday school was organized in a small house — which was used a short time for a hotel — opposite Saint Mary's Hospital, West avenue, and was known as the "West End Sunday school." The classes, scattered throughout the building (one even in the pantry), were under the superintendence of the late Col. John H. Thompson.

In the year 1859 a chapel was built on West avenue, about half way between the places where these schools were held, and the two were united as a Mission school, under the care of Central church. The first session of the school was held in the chapel, January 8, 1860, William S. Bishop, Esq., conducting it.

Mr. George W. Parsons was elected superintendent, and continued in charge till January 19, 1862, the school having a large attendance.

Mr. Parsons, then superintendent of three schools, feeling the need of relief from some of the responsibility, at this time resigned, and Mr. Henry Churchill was elected to fill his place, and held the office till April, 1868, the numbers continuing to increase till often four hundred were present.

During part of the years 1861-2 Rev. Anson Gleason, for many years a successful missionary among the Mohicans of Connecticut, and other Indian tribes, labored in the vicinity and held preaching services and prayer meetings in the chapel.

In October of the year 1867, the Young People's Missionary Society of the Central church, engaged Mrs. L. A. Shepard to act as a city missionary in the the vicinity of West avenue. Her work was very successful — visiting from house to house, holding religious conversation, distributing tracts, etc.

Prayer meetings were held at private houses, conversions were numerous, and thus it seemed necessary that a church should be organized.

Accordingly, on the first Sabbath in April, 1868, eighty-two members of the Central church, then under the pastorate of Rev. S. M. Campbell, D.D., requested letters, and were formerly organized as the Westminster Presbyterian church of Rochester, Rev. F. F. Ellinwood, D.D., assisting in the services of that interesting occasion.

The colony went forth from a sense of duty, trusting in God to sustain and strengthen them. Nor were they disappointed, for, as the result of a revival that year, not only was the number made good to the Central church, but the membership of the new colony was just doubled. The congregation and membership continued to increase, and the prayer meetings, of which five were maintained each week, were generally very interesting. During the summer and fall of 1870 the church worked at a disadvantage, being engaged in building a new edifice. After many delays and some sacrifices, the building was completed and formally dedicated to the service of God, Jan. 26, 1871. Dr. Campbell preached the sermon, taking for his topic, "Tokens of prosperity."

The Central church had shared in the support of its child, and had contributed handsomely toward the building fund, and on the night of the dedication came forward with large gifts to relieve the present necessities. The church was also the recipient of a fine toned memorial bell from one of the elders, and a handsome organ from A. Champion, Esq.

At the end of only three years the Westminster church has risen from a mission chapel to a condition of self-reliance and self-support, with a pleasant, cheerful building, and beautiful Sabbath school room attached, a good congregation, an active, liberal membership, and evidences of the presence of the Holy Spirit in their midst.

The new church went out under the care of Rev. Henry Morey, who is giving his people youthful vigor and hearty earnestness, and whose labor has been very acceptable.

ELDERS.

The first elders were, Messrs. Truman A. Clark and

George M. Mitchell, with the recent addition of Mr. Henry G. Wood.

PASTOR.

Rev. Henry M. Morey was born in West Bloomfield, N. Y.; pursued his preparatory studies at Geneseo academy; graduated at Union college and Princeton seminary; was assistant for the winter of 1865 of the late Dr. J. M. Lowry, in Fort Wayne, Ind.; supplied the church at Pittsford for two years, and came to Rochester in April, 1868.

SUMMARY, JULY 1, 1871.

Pastor—Rev. Henry M. Morey.

Elders—Truman A. Clark, Henry G. Wood, and George M. Mitchell.

S. S. Superintendent—Truman A. Clark.

Number of Teachers—43.

Number of Scholars—375.

Number of Church Communicants—180.

THE REFORMED CHURCH.

An organization with this official name was perfected in the year 1835, with twenty-nine members, of whom the following are still in communion, viz: Mrs. Jane Campbell, John and Elizabeth Boyd, Mrs. Martha Robinson, Mrs. Jane Montgomery, Mrs. Jane Brown, and Mr. John Lowry. The first place of meeting was the High School building, which stood on the site of the Third Presbyterian church, corner of Temple and Lancaster streets. Subsequently an edifice was erected on the corner of Stillson and Main streets, which after occupancy for many years has been sold for business purposes, and the avails applied to erecting one larger, more attractive and commodious, on North St. Paul, near Andrews street.

PASTORS.

Rev. John Fish, of Ireland, a man of great eloquence and pulpit power. He lived but a short time, and is buried at Mount Hope.

Rev. C. B. McKee followed Mr. Fish, in 1835, but resigned in 1842, and has since deceased. His remains now repose in Mount Hope cemetery.

Rev. David Scott was born in a village near Glascow, Scotland; graduated at the University of Glascow and at the Reformed Presbyterian seminary, Paisley, of which the late Dr. Andrew Symington was the distinguished professor; came to America as a licensiate in 1829; was ordained as an evangelist in 1832; was installed pastor of a church at Albany, N.Y., in 1836; assumed the pastorate of the Rochester congregation in 1844, as successor of Rev. Mr. McKee, and after a laborious and eminently successful ministry, demitted his charge in 1862, though still making his home in the city, supplying neighboring pulpits and acting as professor in the Theological seminary at Alllegheny, Pa., till March 29, 1871, when he "fell asleep in Jesus," at the age of seventy-seven years.

> "Servant of Christ, well done;
> Rest from thy lov'd employ:
> The battle fought—the victory won—
> Enter thy Master's joy."

Rev. R. D. Sproule is a native of Allegheny, Pa.; a graduate of Jefferson college, and of Allegheny seminary. After supplying the congregation made vacant by the death of Rev. Mr. Scott, he was unanimously called to the pastorate and installed in 1863, where he now labors with earnest zeal and fidelity among a devoted and prosperous people.

SUMMARY, JULY 1, 1871.

Pastor—Rev. R. D. Sproule.

Elders—Messrs. Hugh Mulholland, Robert Aiton, Hugh Robinson, James Campbell, and Robert Wilson.

Deacons—Messrs. James Aiton, Abraham Errnessie, John Lowry, Thomas S. Lynn, Thomas Percey, John Q. Parks, Thomas A. Gormley, and Samuel G. Robinson.

S. S. Superintendent—Elder Hugh Robinson.

No. of Scholars—88.

No. of Teachers—11.

No. of Communicants—130.

NOTE.—One young man, Rev. John Middleton, a member of this church, after laboring in the ministry at Perth, Canada, Liston, N. Y., Philadelphia, Pa., and Stanton, Ill., has been compelled, through ill health, to suspend his loved employment of preaching the Gospel of Jesus to lost men.

FIRST UNITED CHURCH.

In the spring of 1848, Rev. John VanEaton, of the Associate Reformed Synod, preached three Sabbaths in the school house near Saint Luke's church. Appearances being favorable, Mr. VanEatön remained and held divine services from August, 1848, to May, 1849, in a school house on the corner of Troup street and Plymouth avenue. On the evening of September 21, 1849, an organization was perfected under the title of the First Associate Reformed church of Rochester, with the following named persons as communicants: Robert Bell, Mrs. Martha Bell, Robert Johnson, James and Eliza Reid, William and Janet R. Muir, John Burdock, William Hamilton, Mrs. (Rev.) VanEaton, William and Rachel Hart, Hannah Buddock, Jane Hamilton, Ann and Christina Semple, William and Catherine G. Fisher, Alexander and Mary J. Adams, Alexander and Margaret Blair, and Margaret Hamilton. Of these twenty-three founders, eight are deceased, ten removed to other places, and five are still in communion, viz: Robert and Mrs. Bell, Robert Johnson, William Hart, and Mrs. Margaret Niven.

The first bench of elders was Messrs. William Hamilton, James Reid, William Muir, Robert Bell, and William Leslie.

Rev. John VanEaton installed as first pastor in 1849, remained three years, when ill health compelled him to resign, but not till he had seen "the work of the Lord prosper in his hands."

On the morning of September 8, 1850, the lately reconstructed house of worship on Troup street and Plymouth avenue was consumed by fire, when services were held for four months in the school house on the south side of Allen street, between Fitzhugh and State, and subsequently in a building on the corner of Court and Stone streets (east side), continuing there till 1864, when a purchase was made of the church on Allen street, near Fitzhugh.

Succeeding Rev. Mr. VanEaton was Rev. W. L. McAdams, who was installed June 6, 1854, and resigned after an acceptable and useful pastorate of two years and eight months. Then followed a vacancy of eight months, when Rev. Thomas F. Bond assumed the ministerial charge, and remained four years and five months. Two years then passed away, when the Rev. James P. Sankey, the present incumbent, was inducted into the pastoral office on the 30th of June, 1864; the installation services being conducted by Rev. F. M. Proctor, now of Ohio, Rev. J. VanEaton, of York, and Donald McLaren, D.D., of Geneva. Under the able ministrations and watchful care of their present accomplished, energetic, and faithful leader, this church is taking rank among the strong and influential ecclesiastical bodies of the city.

On the 20th of May, 1868, the Associated Reformed

Presbyterian church, and the Associate Presbyterian church effected an organic union under the title of the "United Presbyterian church of North America," with a total of seven hundred and seventeen churches, and five hundred and forty-one ministers. This consolidation changed the name of this body from the First Associate Reformed church of Rochester, to the United Presbyterian church of Rochester — the name at the head of this chapter.

PASTORS.

Rev. John VanEaton, a native of Xenia, Ohio, and graduate of Miami university, and Oxford (A. R. P.) Theological university of the same State, commenced his pastorate of this church in 1849, continuing until driven away by the ill health of himself and family. Since September 1, 1853, he has been pastor of a large, flourishing and influential church at York, Livingston county, New York.

Rev. W. L. McAdams, pastor here for nearly three years, now resides in Mercer county, Pa., having been obliged to cease preaching on account of ill health.

Rev. Thomas F. Boyd, after a residence here of four and a half years, removed to Pennsylvania, and is pastor of Bethel and Beulah churches in that State.

Rev. James P. Sankey was born in Londonderry, Ohio; pursued his classical studies at Franklin college, and his theological at Allegheny city, Penn.; was licensed to preach in April, 1862, and was placed in charge of this church by the presbytery of Caledonia June 30, 1864. Mr. Sankey is junior pastor of the city, having entered college at fourteen years of age, and commenced preaching at twenty-two.

SUMMARY, JULY 1, 1871.

Pastor—Rev. James P. Sankey.

Elders—Messrs. Robert Bell, Robert Sterrett, Robert Johnson, and Thomas Lisle.

S. S. Superintendent—The pastor.

No. of Scholars—318.

Church Communicants—320.

NOTE.—The enlargement of the present edifice is an absolute necessity. The erection of a new structure being an event, it is hoped, not far distant.

EPISCOPALIAN.

SAINT LUKE'S CHURCH.

The parish of Saint Luke's was organized by the Rev. H. U. Onderdonk, missionary and rector of Saint John's church, Canandaigua, and subsequently Bishop of Pennsylvania, under the corporate title of Saint Luke's church, Genesee Falls. The organization was effected on the 14th of July, 1817, in a school house belonging to Samuel I. Andrews, on the east side of the river, by the election of Colonel Nathaniel Rochester and S. I. Andrews as wardens, and for vestrymen, Silas O. Smith, Roswell Babbitt, John Mastick, Lewis Jenkins, Elisha Johnson, John C. Rochester, William Atkinson, and Oliver Culver.

Occasional services were held for the parish by the Rev. Messrs. Onderdonk, G. H. Norton, A. Welton, and perhaps others, in the school house on the lot adjoining the present church edifice. When Bishop Hobart visited the parish, in September, 1818, he confirmed four persons in the building belonging to the First Presbyterian society, which was kindly loaned for the service. The offer of the original proprietors of "the 100-acre tract," Messrs. Rochester, Fitzhugh and Carroll, to present a lot to the first religious society which would undertake the erection of a church edifice thereon, being still open, the vestry resolved, in July, 1820, to avail themselves of the proposition. A wooden building, thirty-eight by forty-six feet, was immediately reared, and occupied on the following Christmas day. The services of a clergyman had been meanwhile secured, and the Rev. Francis H. Cumming, deacon, entered upon his duties as rector on the first Sunday of December, 1820. On the 20th of February, 1821, the little church was consecrated by Bishop Hobart; and on the following day the rector was advanced to the priesthood.

In April, 1823, the need of a new edifice having become apparent, the vestry determined upon the erection of a stone church, fifty-three by seventy-three feet, the corner-stone of which was laid the same season. The wooden structure was removed to the rear, and served as a Sunday school building until 1832, when it was again removed and converted to other uses. The new church was first occupied on the first Sunday of September, 1825, but, owing to the absence of the bishop in Europe, was not consecrated until September 30, 1826.

The year 1827 was distinguished by the consent of the vestry of Saint Luke's to the organization of a new parish on the east side of the river, to be called Saint Paul's. Fifteen communicants were dismissed to the new parish, and five to a new organization called Trinity church, Penfield.

In 1828 the church was enlarged by the addition of thirty feet to its length, rendering it capable of seating one thousand persons; and a bell was at the same time procured, at a cost of $900.

The Rev. Mr. Cumming resigned the rectorship in March, 1829, after an incumbency of eight years and three months. He was succeeded, December 6, 1829, by the Rev. Henry J. Whitehouse, who was instituted by Bishop Hobart August 29, 1830. In 1832 a Sunday school and lecture room was erected in the rear of the church, forty-four by fifty feet. In the following year a charity school of seventy-five scholars was established, upon the basis of a free school previously in existence, and mainly supported by the Young Ladies' Benevolent Society of Saint Luke's, which continued in active operation until the present common school system was adopted in the city.

During the rector's absence in Europe for a year, from September, 1833, the Rev. James A. Bolles was appointed assistant minister to take charge of the parish; and on the occasion of a later foreign tour, in 1836-37, the Rev. N. F. Bruce, M.D., occupied a similar relation. After a pastorate of marked prosperity and faithfulness, lasting through fourteen years and five months, Dr. Whitehouse resigned, May 1, 1844. On the 9th of May, the Rev. Thomas C. Pitkin was elected rector, and assumed charge of the parish July 14, 1844. He was instituted by Bishop DeLancey August 11 of the same year. The Rev. John N. Norton became assistant to the rector, with the approval of the vestry, in April, 1846. In this year Trinity church was organized, the consent and Godspeed of the vestry of Saint Luke's having been previously given; a large number of the families and communicants of Saint Luke's uniting in the new enterprise. The Rev. Mr. Pitkin, finding his health inadequate to the care of so large a parish, tendered his resignation, to take effect July 12, 1847, after a ministry of three years. In October the vacant rectorship was tendered to the Rev. Henry W. Lee, which he accepted, to enter upon his duties January 1, 1848. The Rev. F. F. Wardwell, deacon, who had been in charge of the parish during the vacancy, remained as the first assistant to the rector. The Rev. Mr. Lee was instituted February 16, 1848, by Bishop DeLancey.

He was subsequently enabled, through the contributions of the Ladies' Missionary Society, to secure the assistance of the Rev. Messrs. Edward Meyer, George H. McKnight, Bethel Judd, D.D., W. H. Barris, George N. Cheney, George W. Watson, and T. A. Hopkins, successively. During his laborious and prosperous ministry of seven years, a new organ replaced the one erected in 1825, and a peal of bells was hung in the tower. The resignation of Dr. Lee was caused by his election to the bishopric of Iowa, which resignation was accepted by the vestry "with unmingled feelings of regret, and with a grateful appreciation of the many qualities which rendered his ministry so important to the prosperity of the parish, and which endeared him to the people of his charge." On Saint Luke's day, the 11th of October, 1854, he was consecrated to the Episcopal office, in the presence of his flock, by Bishops Hopkins, Eastburn, McCoskry, DeLancey, Burgess, and Whitehouse.

In December of the same year the Rev. Benjamin Watson was elected rector, and on the 29th of the ensuing April entered upon his duties; the Rev. T. A. Hopkins having officiated in the interim. Soon after his arrival in the city, he held the primary meeting for the organization of a new parish, chiefly by parishioners of Saint Luke's residing in the south-eastern portion of the city, to be called Christ's church. During the first year of his ministry the church was repaired and improved at a cost of $5,000, a portion of which was provided for by subscription at the time. His institution took place February 14, 1856. He was assisted by the Revs. Robert W. Lewis and C. E. Cheney. After a ministry of four years and three months, considerations of health prompting the Rev. Mr. Watson to dissolve his connection with the church, his resignation was accepted, to take effect August 1, 1859. The Rev. R. Bethell Claxton, D.D., was appointed his successor, and entered upon the rectorship December 1, 1859. On the 20th of the next February the rector was instituted by Bishop DeLancey, Bishop H. W. Lee preaching the sermon. Dr. Claxton was indefatigable in his labors among the poorer members of the parish, and by means derived chiefly from the Sunday school and the Young Ladies' Missionary Society, he succeeded, amid much discouragement, in founding the chapel of the Good Shepherd, in the eleventh ward. He laid the corner-stone of a neat edifice of brick, September 23, 1863; and on the 31st of July of the next year he had the satisfaction of opening the chapel for Divine service. The total cost of the lot and building was upwards of $3000. In the first year of his ministry (August, 1860), a rectory was purchased, upon which $4000 was paid; and in April, 1865, the vestry took order for rebuilding and enlarging the Sunday school accommodations, which work was completed at a cost of $6000, in April, 1866. The assistants of Dr. Claxton were the Revs. Joseph Kidder, Frederick N. Luson, DeWitt C. Loop, Frederick M. Gray, and Horatio Gray His resignation was consequent upon his election to the chair of Professor of Pulpit Eloquence and Pastoral Care in the Divinity school of the Protestant Episcopal church in Philadelphia. It was accepted to take effect October 1, 1865.

The parish, remaining for seven months without a rector, was served by the Rev. W. J. Clark. On the 23d of April, 1866, the Rev. Henry Anstice was elected to the rectorship, which office he still holds, and on the second Sunday of May he entered upon the work. During the same year two lots were added to the rectory grounds, and the interior of the church remodelled and thoroughly refitted in every part. To meet these expenses and liquidate an existing debt, $26,500 were cheerfully subscribed.

While the work was progressing, the congregation worshipped in the First Presbyterian church, through the christian courtesy of its trustees. Saint Luke's was re-opened on the 10th of March, 1867, by the Rt. Rev. A. C. Coxe, D.D., and the institution of the rector followed on the 14th inst., William Pitkin, Esq., presenting the keys of the church, an office he had performed at the institution of every previous rector. The prosperity of the church and its enlarging field of usefulness demanding it, provision was made for an additional assistant minister, and well sustained missionary services were held in various parts of the city. On the 23d of July, 1868, the rector laid the corner-stone of a new chapel, to be built of brick, on Frances street, at the head of Adams. On the 28th of February, 1869, the opening service was held. The building (since named the chapel of the Epiphany), is neatly built, in early English style, sixty by forty-two feet inside, slate roofed, with four double lancet stained glass windows on each side, and a window in front on either side of a central tower, which is eighty-two feet high. The chapel is carpeted and furnished with bell, organ, font, and chancel furniture. The entire cost has been eleven thousand five hundred dollars. An adjoining lot has been secured for a parsonage.

On Easter Monday, 1869, the rector presided at a meeting to incorporate the chapel of the Good Shepherd, as an independent church, and transferred forty-one families and fifty-one communicants from Saint Luke's to form the nucleus of the new parish. The assistants of the present rector have been the Rev. M. R. St.J. Dillon, Jacob Miller, D. H. Lovejoy, W. W. Raymond, and George S. Baker. The last named is still rendering most efficient service in the parish.

RECTORS.

The Rev. Francis H. Cumming, D.D., first rector of Saint Luke's, was born at New Haven, Conn., October 28, 1799. His education was chiefly acquired under the care of the late Dr. Rudd, at Elizabeth, N. J. He was ordained deacon by Bishop Croes, in Saint John's, Elizabeth, in 1819, and was advanced to the priesthood by Bishop Hobart, at Saint Luke's, in February, 1821. His earliest ministry was at Binghamton, whence he was called to Saint Luke's December, 1820. Remaining till March, 1829, he removed to Reading, Pa., and thence to Le Roy, N. Y., spending a year in each place. In 1833 he assumed the secretaryship and general agency for the P. E. S. S. Union in New York, which position he retained four years, at the same time forming and ministering to a congregation on Staten Island. Dissolving his connection with the Sunday School Union, he became first rector of Calvary church, New York. In October, 1839, he accepted the rectorship of Saint Andrew's church, Ann Arbor, Mich. In 1843 he removed to Saint Mark's church, Grand Rapids, where for nearly nineteen years, or until called to the chaplaincy of the Third regiment, Mich. Infantry, he remained. Leaving the army in April, he returned to his family at Grand Rapids, broken in health, and died August 26, 1862.

Rev. Henry John Whitehouse, D.D., LL.D., Oxford and Cantab, is a native of New York city; a graduate of Columbia college and the General Theological seminary; was ordained deacon by Bishop John Croes, D.D., of New Jersey, and priest by Bishop William White, of Pennsylvania; spent two years in Christ's church, Reading, Penn.; came to Rochester in December, 1829; leaving in May, 1844, to assume the rectorship of Saint Thomas' church in his native city, as successor of Dr. Hawks, after declining the presidency of Hobart college, Geneva, the bishopric of Michigan, and several other important posts. In 1851 he went to Illinois, as assistant to Bishop Chase, and upon the death of that venerable prelate, became Episcopal diocesan of Illinois, his residence being Chicago. Bishop Whitehouse visited Europe during 1865 and 1868, traveling extensively, taking an active part in Italian reform, acting for the Bishop of London in visitations of churches in Denmark and Sweden, consecrating a church at Stockholm, and performing other services there and in Russia. Bishop Whitehouse was mainly instrumental in effecting the Lambeth Pan-Anglican Synod, and preached, by invitation of the Archbishop of Canterbury, the opening sermon. He has taken a deep interest in church schools. But during a public life of many years and high honors, no part was characterized by results of greater apparent benefit and marked by a fuller realization of ministerial success, than that of his rectorship of Saint Luke's, in this city. His Lent lectures and Bible class instructions will long live in the grateful recollections of the many who attended upon them through successive years.

The Rev. Thomas Clapp Pitkin, D.D., was born at Farmington, Conn.; graduated at Yale college and the General Theological seminary; ministered at Lawrenceburgh, Ind., and Louisville, Ky., and became rector of Saint Luke's in July, 1844. After a pastorate of three years he went to Trinity church, New Haven, in the relation of associate to the Rev. Dr. Croswell; removed thence to Saint Peter's, Albany, and subsequently became associate with Dr. Shelton at Saint Paul's, Buffalo.

The Right Rev. Henry Washington Lee, D.D., LL.D., Cantab, is a native of Hampden, Conn., but early removed to Springfield, Mass., where his father,

Col. Rosewell Lee, was for forty years superintendent of the United States armory. After a thorough academic education, he was ordained by Bishop Griswold, and for nine years was rector of Christ's church, Springfield. Accepting an invitation to the rectorship of Saint Luke's, he continued in that position until his elevation to the Bishopric of Iowa, in October, 1854, his resignation not taking effect, however, until January, 1855. In the discharge of his Episcopal functions, Dr. Lee has ever been characterized by that single-hearted earnestness and transparent sincerity which marked his earlier ministry. He is the founder, in 1860, of Griswold's college, Davenport, in the theological department of which he fills the chair of Professor of Systematic Divinity; and in 1864 he established the Bishop Lee Female seminary at Dubuque. He was a member of the Lambeth Conference, and received an early decree from Cambridge university.

The Rev. Benjamin Watson, D.D., was born in Philadelphia; graduated at Trinity college and the General Theological seminary. His first parish was Zion church, Newport, R. I., whence he was called to Saint Luke's, in May, 1855. After a rectorship of four years and three months, he accepted a call to the church of the Atonement, Philadelphia, where he still resides.

The Rev. R. Bethel Claxton, D.D., is a native of Philadelphia; graduated at Yale college; pursued his theological studies at the Alexandria seminary, Va. After a rectorship in Pennsylvania and missionary labors in Indiana, he became rector of St. Paul's,

Cleveland, whence he removed to accept the charge of Saint Luke's, in December, 1859. Upon his election to a professorship in the Divinity school, in Philadelphia, he resigned his rectorship, in October, 1865. He is still engaged in the duties of his chair in the Divinity school.

The Rev. Henry Anstice, seventh rector of Saint Luke's, is a native of New York city; a graduate of Williams college, Mass., in 1861, and of the Philadelphia Divinity school, in 1865. He was ordained deacon in July and presbyter in November, of the same year, by Bishop Potter, of New York. He officiated at Irvington, on the Hudson, until his acceptance of a call to Saint Luke's, in April, 1866. He entered upon the discharge of his duties in this relation on the second Sunday in May, and, after five years of labor, is still the rector of this church.

Among the young men who went from this church into the ministry were:

Rev. Kendrick Metcalf, D.D., Professor in Hobart college, Geneva.

Rev. William Stanton, D.D., residing in New York.

Rev. Erastus Spalding, who died in Vienna, N. Y., leaving four sons, all now in the ministry.

Rev. Jeremiah H. Waldo, Springfield, Illinois.

Rev. Charles B. Stout, Chicago, Illinois.

Rev. William T. Aitkins, deceased.

Rev. W. H. Hickcox, Leroy, Kansas.

Rev. Ethan Allen, deceased.

Rev. Henry Lockwood (missionary to China), Pittsford, N. Y.

Rev. T. R. Chipman, deceased.

BAPTISMS, CONFIRMATIONS AND CONTRIBUTIONS DURING FIFTY YEARS.

Rev. F. H. Cumming, D.D., Dec., 1820, to March, 1829.
Bap., 255; conf., 110; cont., $14,500.

Rev. H. J. Whitehouse, D.D., Dec., 1829, to May, 1844.
Bap., 1167; conf., 444; cont., $17,094.

Rev. T. C. Pitkin, July, 1844, to July, 1847.
Bap., 234; conf., 97; cont., $5,140.

Rev. H. W. Lee, D.D., January, 1848, to January, 1855.
Bap., 588; conf., 189; cont., $20,431.

Rev. B. Watson, May, 1855, to August, 1859.
Bap., 263; conf., 76; cont., $15,448.

Rev. B. Claxton, D.D., Dec., 1859, to Oct., 1865.
Bap., 403; conf., 127; cont., $23,957.

Rev. Henry Anstice, May, 1866, to May, 1871.
Bap., 418; conf., 298; cont., $92,209.

Several brief interims.
Bap., 79; conf., 5; cont., $631.

Total of baptisms, 3407.
Total of confirmations, 1346.
Total contributions, $189,410.

SUMMARY, JULY 1, 1871.

Rector—Rev. Henry Anstice.

Wardens—Messrs. William Brewster and Gilman H. Perkins.

Vestrymen—Messrs. E. Darwin Smith, E. E. Sill, James Brackett, William Eastwood, Charles H. Chapin, Edward W. Williams, Charles F. Smith, and Thomas Raines.

Clerk of Vestry—Thomas Raines.

Treasurer—Edward R. Hammatt.

S. S. Superintendent—Rector.

S. S. Scholars—397.

Communicants—614.

SAINT PAUL'S CHURCH.

This second Episcopal parish in Rochester was originally organized under the title of Saint Paul's church, the edifice bearing that name being erected in 1829. In architectural design, this structure was far in advance of anything at that time in Western New York; its beauty and grandeur drawing to it visitors from all the country around. Its spire was designed to exceed in height anything in this part of the State; but after successful raising and during the absence of workmen at dinner, the elements made sport of their ambition, and they returned to find that the wind had cleaned it even with the roof. The original design was abandoned and the present tower substituted. As a key to important features in its subsequent history, it may be remarked that a loan of $10,000 from the North River Insurance Company was effected by the vestry, to be used as part of the building fund, which was secured by a mortgage on the building.

Rev. Charles P. McIlvaine (now the venerable Bishop of Ohio) was the presbyter presiding at the meetings for the organization of the parish; Rev. F. H. Cumming being rector of Saint Luke's.

"The leading men at the organization and for many

years afterward (writes an old parishioner), were Messrs. William Atkinson and Elisha Johnson. For many years Saint Paul's was called Johnson's church, he being the leading spirit in the enterprise."

The first rector was Rev. Sutherland Douglas, of whom an extended notice from another hand will be found at the close of this narrative.

He was succeeded by Rev. Chauncey Colton, who left on account of ill health, in 1832, and is now a resident of Maryland.

Rev. H. V. D. Johns was called early in 1832. Of him the same friend writes: "He visited the parish in Lent of that year, accepted a call, preached on Sunday, baptized an adult, and left for Baltimore for his family, but did not return." This adult was for fifteen years after a most exemplary and useful worker in the parish, and during some of its darkest days the faithful steward of its finances.*

Then came Rev. Burton H. Hickox from Palmyra, who was in charge from 1832 to 1835 — being remarkable for prudence, persistence and success in relieving parishes from financial embarassments, and instituting plans of well doing.

In 1835 Rev. Orange Clark, D. D., was called from Lockport, and continued in charge four years, when he removed to California and died.

Rev. Washington VanZandt became rector in April, 1839. It was a period of special religious interest in the city, and Mr. VanZandt " was for six months (one of) the most popular ministers the church in Rochester

---

* Ansel Roberts, Esq.

had ever had." At the first visit of Bishop DeLancey thirty-one persons were confirmed and at another seventeen. After a pastorate of one year and six months he resigned. The history of this period was one of disaster to the parish and to the sacred interests parishes are designed to further. Let a veil be drawn over it. But it would be a crime against the uses of history not to record here the fact that during this incumbency peremptory inhibition was laid upon the amusement of dancing, in the case of young persons coming to confirmation or to the holy communion in this parish.

After a long vacancy, when the pulpit was supplied by professors from Geneva, the Rev. William E. Eigenbrodt (now professor in General Episcopal seminary, N. Y., and secretary of convention), was called from Bainbridge, W. N. Y., and entered upon his duties June 12, 1842, continuing till December, 1843, when he resigned; but not without inaugurating means for rescuing the parish property from its anomalous condition, in its transfer from the ownership of individuals to that of the bishop of the diocese, and this with a view to its restoration ultimately to the legal guardianship of a vestry; a result in the end happily accomplished.

The rectorship of Mr. Eigenbrodt was marked by the happiest and most satisfactory relations with the vestry and the parish; but it had this special and crowning glory, that it restored in all minds, at a most critical moment, that reverence for the sacred office which had received so disastrous a shock; and that it re-established as the true measure of admiration and support towards a christian pastor, the standard of exemplary purity and fidelity in character, and of the solid qualities of the shepherd, guide and teacher.

Under the rectorship of the Rev. B. H. Hickox, the church edifice had been rescued from menaced alienation, and the title to the church property had passed to a new corporation, taking the name of Grace church. This new corporation effected a settlement with the old creditor, the insurance company, by purchasing the edifice under a foreclosure of the mortgage. The corporation of Trinity church, New York, contributed a liberal sum to enable Grace church to compass this settlement, taking a mortgage on the edifice.

In the end there was a second foreclosure; and the edifice was bought in under it by the association of gentlemen who held the title during the two rectorships last named; and who had besides made large advances to carry on the parish.

It was to eradicate the bitter root of original debt, against which he felt it hopeless for any pastor to contend, and of which he was ignorant when he entered upon the charge, that Mr. Eigenbrodt resolved to bring things to a crisis by resigning the charge.

Bishop DeLancey made, in October, 1844, this record of the facts:

"February 4 to 11.—I visited Rochester on this occasion with especial reference to the affairs of Grace church, worshiping in Saint Paul's church edifice; which edifice had been bought in under a foreclosure, by a few members of the congregation, some of whom had been large contributors to the church before, and who advanced the requisite amount in the hope that the church might be revived and themselves refunded. The rector had resigned on account of the pecuniary embarrassments of the church. The vestry were unable to purchase the church, and there was apprehension lest the building should, by the force of circumstances, be alienated from the Episcopal church, and the congregation dispersed.

"I deemed it my duty, after consulting with wise and influential lay friends in Rochester, to become the proprietor of the edifice, in the hope of thus ensuring to the church in perpetuity the possession of the building, in case the effort to relieve it from pecuniary embarassment should succeed, and also to afford a basis for the experiment to relieve it to be fairly tried.

"The congregation with the vestry of Grace church continue to worship in this church, supplied with the ministrations of the clergy laboring in it under my direction, and awaiting the result of the experiment, as well as in aiding in the effort to rescue the church from its difficulties.

"The funds derived from pew rents are applied to providing the services of the clergy, to the payment of the interest on the debt and reduction of the principal, and to the contingent expenses. My own services are given gratuitously, and are designed to be rendered in such way and at such times as not to interfere with my diocesan duties, which are paramount."

The experiment was blessed with success, and in the end the title to the edifice was placed, free of incumbrance, in the corporation of Grace church, where it remains.

The clergymen employed under this arrangement were, (1) Rev. Stephen Douglas, for three months; (2) Rev. John V. VanIngen, D.D., who was soon joined by Rev. Charles H. Platt, deacon, both being appointed missionaries for city and county without stipends, giving also gratuitous services to Penfield, Brighton, Pittsford, &c. Others were added as assistants to the working staff in all parts of the city and suburbs. Besides the rector, Rev. Mr. Platt, there ministered to this parish, Rev. John N. Norton, Rev. Jonathan L. Eaton, Rev. Walter Ayrault (now D.D.), Rev. T. N. Benedict, Rev. Joshua Smith, Rev. Sylvanus Reed, Rev. Wentworth L. Childs, Rev. W. H. Barris, Rev. Philemon E. Coe, Rev. Albert Wood, and Rev. John B. Calhoun.

The rescue of the parish property from encumbrance, happily effected in 1847, was in part the effort of the bishop, who secured about two thousand dollars for this purpose, and of vestry and parishioners, with the noble zeal and activity of young men who gave here their first services in the ministry with a devotion to humble labor among the poor never to be forgotten for fidelity and success.

The title to the property being now in the vestry the parish, freed from debt, entered upon a career of quiet, steady growth and usefulness. Rev. Dr. VanIngen was chosen rector at a salary of one thousand dollars (1848); of which he remitted two hundred dollars in consideration of the recent exhausting efforts of the parish.

The church edifice was destroyed by fire on a Sunday morning, in July, 1847. There being an insurance of ten thousand dollars and no debt, the vestry proceeded courageously to rebuild. Services were held for a time in the old high school, until Christmas, 1847, when the restored basement was joyfully occupied. The entire edifice being completed, was consecrated as Grace church, December 17, 1848.

Upon the removal of Dr. VanIngen to Saint Pauls, Minnesota, in 1854, his place was taken by Rev. Maunsell VanRensselaer, D.D., who, after an administration of characteristic fidelity, was called to the presidency of DeVeaux college, Niagara Falls.

He was succeeded by the present rector, Rev. Israel Foote, D.D., in May, 1859. Under his laborious, prudent and faithful administration, the parish has grown to its present condition. A parsonage (original cost ten thousand dollars), and a parish school building (twelve thousand dollars), have been added to its property, and the church edifice enlarged, improved and beautified, at a cost of twenty-seven thousand dollars. Let not the record be omitted that (while in the language of the present rector, "None of us do anything to boast of, and why it should be paraded before the world but to shame us, I know not," to all of which the present writer subscribes), not one dollar of this was raised by fairs, or "any means except direct subscription, bequest or contribution."

The communicants reported by Dr. Eigenbrodt in 1843, were 108, but now they number 464. But no eye but that of the All-seeing, and no measure but that of the final judgement can give report of the influence or the actual result of the life of an individual or of a parish. And in view of the actual state of morals to-day, no demonstration, one would think, so well becomes "the churches," as that of humiliation in sack-cloth and ashes. J. V. V. I.

NOTE.—During one of the interims of rectorship, about the year 1831, the members of the First Presbyterian church worshiped for several months in this church, while their's was undergoing repair. An act of courtesy gratefully appreciated, and an illustration of christian unity, of which this city has often been the scene.

Rev. Sutherland Douglas, son of the late Alanson Douglas, of Troy, was born in 1804; graduated at Yale college and the General Theological seminary; was ordained deacon by Bishop Griswold; accepted charge of Saint John's church, D. C.; became first rector of Saint Paul's, Rochester, in 1828, but resigned in less than a year on account of impaired health. He sailed to Havre in hopes of restoration, but after severe illness died in London, after a brief but devoted ministerial career. During the few lucid hours of his last sickness, he received the sacrament from Rev. Dr. Wilson (subsequently Metropolitan of India), who had his remains deposited in his family vault at Islington, there to await the resurrection of the just. More than forty years have passed away and yet the writer of this sketch, young then, well remembers the text of one of his discourses, and vividly recalls his plaintive voice, deeply serious countenance, and earnest manner, in the sacred desk.

> "The loveliest star of evening's train
> Sets early in the western main;
> The brightest star of morning's host,
> Scarce ris'n in brighter beams is lost."

William B. Douglas, Esq., of this city, is a brother, and Mrs. Samuel Miller, of New Haven, a sister of this young and gifted divine.

SUMMARY, JULY 1, 1871.

Rector—Rev. Israel Foote, D.D.

Assistant Rector—Rev. C. N. Allen.

Wardens—Messrs. George W. Mumford and Johnson I. Robins.

Vestrymen—Messrs. George Ellwanger, George E. Mumford, H. F. Atkinson, F. Goodrich, R. S. Kenyon, D. A. Watson, F. L. Durand, and E. K. Warren.

S. S. Superintendent—The rector.

Librarian—Bernard S. VanIngen.

No. of S. S. Scholars—305.

No. of Communicants—464.

TRINITY CHURCH.

The organization of a third Episcopal church and parish in the city of Rochester, and in that portion of the city commonly called Frankfort, occupied the thoughts and enlisted the sympathy of the Rev. Dr. Henry J. Whitehouse, then rector of Saint Luke's church, and now the distinguished Bishop of Illinois, as early as the year 1836. The project met with the sympathy and coöperation of several prominent and influential members of Dr. Whitehouse's parish, and subscriptions were made for the object to the amount of about one thousand dollars. A lot was purchased opposite Brown's square, and, realizing that the foundations of parochial strength are securely laid in Sunday schools, Seth C. Jones, Esq., an earnest layman and parishioner of Saint Luke's church, opened a Sunday school in the district school house that then stood on the square. Here the work seems to have rested until, in 1844, Dr. Whitehouse received and accepted a call to the rectorship of Saint Thomas's church, New York. The prosecution of the enterprise that lay so near his heart was a prominent subject of his exhortations to the attached and beloved people of his flock as he bade them farewell, and urged them to enlarge their boundaries and multiply their activities for the good, not of the parish simply, but of the church at large.

Dr. Whitehouse was succeeded by the Rev. Thomas C. Pitkin, of Louisville, Ky., whose influence was cheerfully lent to the realization of his predecessor's wishes. During the month of August, 1845, the subscribers to the fund above mentioned, together with other friends of the movement, and under the official sanction and direction of the Rev. Mr. Pitkin, met in the public school house number five, corner of Fish (now Centre) and Jones streets, and began public services Sunday afternoons and evenings, Mr. Pitkin, the Rev. Dr. VanIngen, then rector of Saint Paul's church, and others, officiating at their convenience.

On the 27th of October following a meeting was held at the same place, and the legal organization of a new parish, to be called "Trinity church," was effected by the election of Messrs. Henry E. Rochester and Seth C. Jones as wardens, and Messrs. George R. Clark, Samuel F. Witherspoon, George Arnold, David Hoyt, Patrick G. Buchan, William E. Lathrop, Lewis P. Beers, and Seth M. Maltby as vestrymen. On the 22d of December following the Rev. Vandervoort Bruce, of New York, was called to the rectorship of the new parish, and having accepted the call he preached his first sermon to the little flock January 8, 1846. The following day, at a meeting convened for the purpose, it was resolved to sell the lot already owned on Brown street, and to purchase what was considered a more eligible one, on the corner of Fish and Frank streets. Seth C. Jones, Henry E. Rochester, and George Arnold were appointed a building committee, and they at once procured plans for a church edifice from D. C. McCollum, architect, and contracted with William Bassett for building the same. Subscriptions were made and the work progressed so well that on the 14th of June following the corner-stone of the church was laid in the presence and with the assistance of the city clergy, the rector making the address.

On the 24th of December following, it being Christmas Eve, divine service was held in the church for the first time, the rector preaching the sermon, and the Rev. Fortune C. Brown, of Avon, and the Rev. W. Ayrault, of Canandaigua, assisting in the service. Previous to this date the services had been held in public school house number five, under great and manifest disadvantages, but so strong was the faith and so earnest the labors of this handful of parishioners that a spiritual harvest had been made ready to the laborer's hand, in a few months. The holy eucharist was celebrated for the first time February 2d of this year, when twenty-two of the faithful communicated. The sacrament of holy baptism was first administered March 8th, the candidate being Edward, the infant son of S. F. Witherspoon, Esq. The holy rite of confirmation was first administered August 23d, by Bishop DeLancey, to nineteen persons. Meantime a Sunday school had been organized, and was successfully conducted under Henry E. Rochester, Esq., as superintendent, and Mrs. George Arnold, assistant superintendent.

The Rev. Mr. Bruce resigned the rectorship of the parish May 12, 1847, after a ministry of but sixteen months, and removed to New York city, where he still resides. He was succeeded by the Rev. Charles D. Cooper, of Wilkesbarre, Pa., who entered upon the discharge of his duties October 1st, the same year. Under his ministry the parish interests continued to thrive, and on the morning of February 15, 1848, the debt having been entirely paid, the church was consecrated to the worship of Almighty God. Bishop DeLancey was the consecrator, and there were of the reverend clergy present and assisting, besides the rector, the Revs. Henry W. Lee, D.D., then rector of Saint Luke's, Rochester, and now Bishop of Iowa, J. V. VanIngen, D.D., S. Benedict, Mason Gallagher, A. P. Stryker, J. A. Bolles, A. Lockwood, and Samuel Chipman. Two days later the rector was formally instituted into his cure, and forty-five laymen communicated. Mr. Cooper labored faithfully among his people, but his ministry was even shorter than his predecessor's, for on the 10th of December, 1849, he accepted a call to Philadelphia, where he still resides, in charge of the church and parish of the Holy Apostles.

Mr. Cooper was succeeded by the Rev. Robert J. Parvin, of Towanda, Pa., who assumed the rectorship February 10th. His first sermon is still most distinctly remembered by his hearers, not only on account of the interest which usually attaches to such occasions, but also on account of the singular pertinency of his text, "I ask therefore for what intent ye have sent for me." Mr. Parvin had a successful, though short ministry in this parish, and resigned August 12, 1852, to take charge of a parish in Pittsfield, Mass. Subsequently he became an agent of the "Society for the Increase of the Ministry," and was among those who perished on board of the ill fated steamer United States, which was burned on the Ohio, December, 1868.

It will thus be seen that from the outset the parish had to contend against an evil that still obtains in the church everywhere, a constant change in the pastorate. But there were stout hearts and generous deeds among the laity which were an abundant earnest of ultimate success. The records of those days tell the same unvarying tale of self-sacrifice for Christ, and when the standard of pecuniary values is compared with that of the present, the donations of those early members of the parish toward its constant and increasing enterprises, seem truly munificent.

There is an almost irresistible temptation to particularize somewhat on this head, and we are restrained only by the knowledge that those earnest churchmen — many of them still with us — are characterized by too genuine a modesty to tolerate any mention of their generosity other than in general items.

During the ministry of Mr. Parvin the chancel window was completed, and a Sunday school room fitted up for week day services and lectures.

Mr. Parvin was succeeded, October 1, 1852, by the Rev. Addison B. Atkins, of Oswego, N. Y., who remained until June 12, 1854, when he removed to a wider field of usefulness. At his last celebration of the Eucharist, one hundred and five communicated, a sufficient evidence of growth in things spiritual. Mr. Atkins is now rector of Saint John's church, Georgetown, D. C.

On the 5th of September following, a call was extended to the Rev. George N. Cheney, of Penn Yan, N. Y., who entered upon his work October 1. His ministry, which was the longest one ever exercised by any of the rectors of this parish, lasted until May 1, 1863, when failing health and sundry private considerations admonished him to retire from the care of active parochial life. Entering upon his work with an eye single to his Master's glory, and with a zeal which, though sometimes "cast down," could never be "destroyed," he left a most enduring record in the hearts of his people. During the great rebellion he secured temporary leave of absence from the parish, that he might carry the word and sacraments of the church to the soldiers who were fighting for the nation's life, and in the capacity of chaplain to the 33d regiment, New York Volunteers, he served the Master and his fellows most faithfully. Retiring to the country to rest at the house of a friend, he died June 12, 1863. The parish he served so well has erected a mural tablet above the altar and on the the sanctuary wall, with the appropriate inscription, "A Beloved Brother and Faithful Minister in the Lord."

The parish had now realized such a measure of material prosperity that it became necessary to mature plans for the enlargement of the church edifice. Hitherto the body of the church consisted of a nave and transepts, the whole outline describing a cross. Plans were submitted and adopted at a vestry meeting, held June 16, 1863, for enlarging the church by extending the side walls ten feet on either side, thus adding two rows of pews and two aisles to the already existing nave. These plans were adopted, the church was enlarged and thoroughly refurnished, and an accrued debt of a considerable amount was paid off, thus placing the parish on a good financial footing. On the 9th of next November, a call was extended to the Rev. John W. Clark, of Brooklyn, N. Y., and on the 6th of December, he took charge of the parish as rector. He remained only until November 13, 1864, when he resigned, and accepted a call to Saint Thomas's church, Dover, N. H.

On the 24th of the following April, a call was extended to the Rev. John V. VanIngen, D.D., formerly of Saint Paul's church, and sometimes doing mission work in Minnesota, who accepted, and at once took charge of the parish. He remained until July 1, 1868, when he resigned, and became agent of the "Society for the Increase of the Ministry." A vacancy in the rectorship of eight months now occurred, which, together with other preëxisting causes not necessary to be mentioned, operated disastrously on the interests of the parish, and confident predictions were made that its race was run. Families which had ever filled its pews and swelled its income, contributing to its material and spiritual strength, had become scattered, and only a faithful few remained to constitute the semblance of a parish. But the faith of those few never wavered, and in response to their call, the Rev. Charles H. W. Stocking, rector of Christ's church, Ansonia, Conn., took charge of the parish March 1, 1869. Seldom is a call accepted under more discouraging circumstances. The exterior and original portion of the church had fallen somewhat into decay, while the interior had become still more unseemly. There was no choir, scarcely any parishoners, and little more than income enough to pay the sexton. A volunteer chorus choir was formed and rehearsed by the rector, the Sunday school was re-organized, with the assistance of its constant benefactor, S. F. Witherspoon, Esq., and general measures of improvement inaugurated. A fund of about three thousand dollars was raised for improvements within and without the church building, and on the 11th of July, it was re-opened by the Right Rev. A. Cleaveland Coxe, D.D., bishop of the diocese, who preached and administered the holy rite of confirmation to twenty-two persons.

This brings the history of the parish down to the present time. During the two years rectorship of the present incumbent, the parish has been making rapid strides forward in the part of material and religious progress, and its future seems reasonably secure. Its membership, income and influence are largely beyond what it has ever before enjoyed; a result attributable more to the zeal and coöperation of its members, than to the labors or deserts of its rector.

During the present incumbency a parish Guild has been organized, the members of which are solemnly pledged:

1. To aid in the reverent performance of divine worship, by preparing and keeping in order the vestments of the clergy and all other appointments of the choir, the vestry-room and the chancel.

2. To be present before, during, and after all public services, when not providentially and absolutely

prevented, and to so order the above appointments as to secure a more seemly and reverent respect for the house of God.

3. To inculcate by precept and example the duty of reverence for the holy place.

4. To seek out and report to the rector any existing cases of sickness, suffering or destitution within their respective districts, and, under his direction, to aid such as are worthy.

5. To ascertain and report to the rector the names of all strangers moving within the parish, and who attend its services and unite with them in facilitating an early and cordial acquaintance with those "who are of the same household of faith."

This institution has accomplished much good to the parish and the city.

A parish school was also opened last year under the immediate supervision of the rector, and with Miss Frances M. Buchan, an earnest and most efficient teacher, as principal.

The Sunday school is an element of great strength. It numbers eighteen teachers, and two hundred and fifty scholars.

Of the original incorporators but four remain within the parish, viz: George R. Clark, S. F. Witherspoon, George Arnold and Dr. B. F. Gilkeson.

The present incumbent, Rev. Charles H. W. Stocking, was born in Norwich, Conn.; at the age of sixteen he removed to Providence, and thence to Boston, where he prepared for college. He entered Trinity college, Hartford, in 1856, graduated in 1860, entered the General Theological seminary, New York city, where he also graduated. Ordained to the deaconate by Bishop Horatio Potter, in New York, June 28, 1863, and to the priesthood by the same bishop, at Brion Cliff, Westchester county, N. Y., December 17, 1863, of which parish he had the charge for the first year of his ministry. In October, 1864, he became rector of the church of the Nativity, Bridgeport, Conn., and warden of the orphanage connected with the same. In October, 1865, he accepted the rectorship of Christ's church, Ansonia, Conn. In connection with the parent parish, he also founded mission parish at Nichols' Farms, Trumball, Conn., which, in four years, became self-supporting, and was placed under the charge of a resident pastor.

In March, 1869, he removed to Rochester, where he now holds the rectorship of Trinity parish.

STATISTICS OF THE PARISH.

Since its formation, 808 have been baptized, 341 confirmed, 247 couples united in holy matrimony, and 378 persons buried.

The parish at present numbers more than 700 souls, of whom about 250 are communicants.

Of those who found in Trinity church a spiritual mother, six have gone forth as priests of Christ's church to minister the word and sacraments to others.

Of the eight priests who have served at its altar, two now rest from their labors, the Revs. G. N. Cheney and Robert J. Parvin.

The Rev. Vandervoort Bruce is living in New York city, and is without any parochial care.

CHURCHES OF ROCHESTER. 111

Rev. Charles D. Cooper is rector of the church of the Holy Apostles, Philadelphia.

Rev. Addison B. Atkins is rector of Saint John's church, Georgetown, D. C.

Rev. John W. Clark is rector of Saint Paul's church, East Saginaw, Mich.

Rev. J. V. VanIngen, D.D., is chaplain of the House of Refuge, Rochester.

SUMMARY, JULY 1, 1871.

Rector—Rev. Charles H. W. Stocking.

Wardens—Messrs. George Arnold and Chauncey W. Clarke.

Vestrymen—Messrs. William F. Holmes, James Brown, R. D. Kellogg, Virgil C. Goodwin, Dwight Knapp, James W. Kelly, Sylvester P. Robins, E. Henry Scrantom, and F. G. Ranney, clerk.

S. S. Superintendent—Rector.

Assistant Superintendent—S. F. Witherspoon.

No. of Scholars—250.

No. of Communicants—250.

CHRIST'S CHURCH.

Recognizing the necessity of another Episcopal church on the east side of the river, several prominent members of Saint Luke's church, together with a few from Grace church, obtaining the consent of the rectors of the city parishes, met and organized, with the following officers: Silas O. Smith and David Hoyt, wardens (both deceased); Andrew J. Brackett, D. B. Beach, D. M. Dewey, John Fairbanks, J. M. Winston, Charles R. Babbitt, Delos Wentworth, and Edward M. Smith, vestrymen.

The first services of the newly organized parish were held in Palmer's Hall, on Sunday, April 29, 1855, the Rev. Benjamin Watson, of Saint Luke's, officiating. Upon nomination of Bishop DeLancey, the Rev. Henry A. Neely, of Utica, now Bishop of Maine, was elected rector of the parish.

Mr. Neely continued the rectorship until the autumn of 1862, when, to the great regret of those among whom he had labored so earnestly for seven years, he resigned the parish, and accepted the chaplaincy of Hobart college, Geneva.

He was succeeded by Rev. Anthony Schuyler, D.D., of Saint John's church, Oswego, and during his efficient ministry the congregation steadily increased. His health requiring a change of climate, he accepted a call to Grace church, Orange, New Jersey, in 1867.

The third rector of the church is Walton W. Battershall, of Ravenswood, Long Island, the present incumbent.

The favorable location of the church, and the energy and enterprise which, through all its history, have characterized the parish, have, by the grace of God, given it an almost unprecedented growth, and made it an efficient instrument of christian work. During the pastorate of its first rector the church was enlarged to double its previous capacity, and a chapel for the Sunday school was built, adjoining the church. Under the rectorship of the Rev. Dr. Schuyler a tower was added to the church edifice. Within the last two years extensive improvements have been made in the interior of the church, and a rectory has been built on the lot adjoining the church lawn.

In June, 1870, by the advice and support of several laymen, the Rev. Mr. Battershall called the Rev. Daniel Flack, formerly of the cathedral of Our Merciful Saviour, at Fairbault, Minn., to take the charge of the parish school and the mission work of the parish in the twelfth ward.*

* In June, 1871, the mission, with the cordial consent and favor of the vestry of Christ's church, became an independent parish, under the name of Saint Clement's church and the rectorship of the Rev. Daniel Flack. A valuable lot has been purchased, and measures are being taken for the erection of a church edifice during the coming year.

RECTORS.

Rev. Henry Adams Neely, D.D., was born at Fayetteville, N. Y.; was educated at Jubilee college, Illinois, and Hobart college, Geneva, where he received his academic titles of A.M. and D.D.; was ordained priest in Calvary church, Utica, June 18, 1854, of which church he was assistant rector for nearly three years, when he accepted a call to become first rector of Christ's church, Rochester, in August, 1855, of which parish he retained the charge for seven years, when he was appointed first chaplain of his *alma mater* at Geneva. From that position he became assistant minister of Trinity church, New York, with the charge of Trinity chapel, and finally was elected second Bishop of Maine, and was consecrated June 25, 1867. Untiring industry with ardent zeal and devotion to his calling have carried Dr. Neely onward step by step to the highest position in the church of which he is a worthy diocesan. His residence is Portland, Maine.

Rev. Anthony Schuyler, D.D., is a native of Seneca, Ontario county, N. Y.; a graduate of Hobart college, Geneva; and practiced law for ten years. His theological studies were pursued under the direction of Dr. Walker, of Ithaca. His first rectorship was at Penn Yan; then at Oswego for ten years; when he came to Rochester as second rector of Christ's church, being installed October 1, 1862, and resigning July 1, 1868, to the regret of his parishioners, and assumed a pastorate at Orange, N. J., which position he now holds with the same ability and acceptance that characterized him here and elsewhere.

Rev. Walton W. Battershall was born at Troy, N.Y.; graduated at Yale college in 1864, and at the General Theological seminary, New York, in 1867; was for a year and a half assistant minister of Zion church, in that city, and in 1868 accepted the rectorship of Saint Thomas's church, Ravenswood, L. I., whence he removed to Rochester, and was installed rector of Christ's church January 1, 1869, which important post he now holds with the cordial unanimity of the parish, which, during his administration, has increased by one-half its present number of communicants.

SUMMARY, JULY 1, 1871.

Rector—Rev. Walton W. Battershall.

Wardens—Delos Wentworth, Edward M. Smith.

Vestrymen—C. E. Upton, D. M. Dewey, A. Burbank, J. H. Nellis, W. H. Shepard, W. J. Ashley, J. Moreau Smith, Curtis Clark, Charles W. Hardy, clerk.

S. S. Superintendent—William J. Ashley.

No. of Communicants—410.

S. S. Teachers—26.

S. S. Scholars—200.

Report of mission not included in above.

GOOD SHEPHERD.

During the pastorate of the Rev. Dr. Claxton, rector of Saint Luke's (in 1863-4), a mission of that parish was established, and a chapel built on Grape street. On the 3d of March, 1869, this was organized as a separate parish, by the Rev. Henry Anstice, successor of Dr. Claxton, under the title of the church of the Good Shepherd. The first wardens were Messrs. John Greenwood and George Cummings. The first vestrymen were Messrs. Thomas Thompson, Thomas Tamblingson, William Attridge, Jr., Samuel Attridge, C. H. Finch, Robert G. Newman, William Webb, and Walter Williamson.

RECTORS.

Rev. Jacob Miller, resigned September 1, 1869.

Rev. J. Newton Spear, resigned on account of ill health. Resides at Altoona, Pa.

Rev. James S. Barnes, came from and returned to Brooklyn.

Rev. Frederick Walter Raikes, a native of England and a student in Germany. After having a pastoral charge at Tonawanda, N. Y., and being an assistant minister of Grace church, Lockport, he was ordained to the priesthood by Bishop Coxe, and installed rector of the church of the Good Shepherd.

SUMMARY, JULY 1, 1871.

Rector—Rev. Frederick Walter Raikes.

Wardens—John W. Greenwood, George Cummings.

Vestrymen—Messrs. Robert G. Newman, Thomas Thompson, Thomas Tamblingson, William Attridge, Jr., William Webb, Thomas Baxendale, George Thorn, and Samuel Attridge.

S. S. Superintendent—Rector, assisted by John W. Greenwood.

No. of S. S. Scholars—145.

No. of Communicants—30.

METHODIST.

FIRST, ASBURY, NORTH STREET, ALEXANDER STREET, CORNHILL, FRANK STREET, GERMAN, ZION.

Methodism has been quaintly though not inaptly styled "religion on horse-back," being the pioneer corps of the sacramental army. When Wesley and his associates forsook the social attractions and scholastic halls of London and Oxford, to "preach Christ and Him crucified" to the miners of Cornwall, Newcastle, and like semi-barbaric regions of England and Wales, they exemplified what was in their minds to be the characteristic feature of the society they established. As a rare exception, Methodists were in Rochester preceded by Presbyterians and Episcopalians. This arose from the fact that the pioneer immigrants were from New England and Maryland, and brought with them their religious sentiments and their ecclesiastical forms of worship.

The first Methodist meeting was held in June, 1817, in the dwelling house of Fabritius Reynolds, which stood near to the intersection of Fitzhugh street with Buffalo street, the service being conducted by Elder Elisha House.

These informal services were held in private dwellings and school houses up to September 20, 1820, when the First Methodist Episcopal church of Rochester was organized, with the following trustees: Messrs. Frederick Clark, Abelard Reynolds, Elam Smith, Dan. Rowe, and Nathaniel Draper. The edifice first erected stood on the corner of South St. Paul street, the lot being presented by Messrs. Elisha Johnson and Enos Stone. The building committee were Messrs. N. Draper, B. Hall, and R. Beach. The size and locality of this structure became so inadequate and inconvenient that it was resolved to erect a building with more room, to accommodate the increasing attendance, and nearer the center of population. As the result of such united purpose, but with very large pecuniary sacrifice, the massive and spacious stone edifice was erected on the corner of Fitzhugh and Buffalo streets. This sanctuary was dedicated to the worship of Jehovah in the fall of 1831, but on the 5th of January, 1835, became a mass of burned and unsightly ruins. There being no insurance, the loss was peculiarly heavy and depressing. But the public sympathy was deeply awakened, which expressed itself in the influx of money and other donations sufficient to rebuild at once, and another of great attractiveness took its place, and stood till the land was sold, and another structure was built a little to the north; the dedication sermon being preached by Rev. Dr. Reid, then president of Genesee college, Lima.

A division of the society being deemed advisable, another organization was formed September 26, 1836, and a church edifice of stone erected on the corner of Main and Clinton streets, which was dedicated in

February, 1843; the officiating clergymen being Rev. Drs. John Dempster and Samuel Luckey. This society was afterwards merged in the Asbury M. E. church, which was organized under its new and present name February 1, 1860. Great improvements have recently been made in the audience room of the building, rendering it very commodious and attractive.

In March, 1852, Aristarchus Champion, Esq., gave to the Methodist denomination $10,000, to be used in building four church edifices in the suburbs of the city. Of this generous sum $2,000 were donated to aid in erecting the North street church, near the corner of North and Hudson streets, which was dedicated November 2, 1853; the sermon being preached by Rev. Schuyler Seager, D.D. This ecclesiastical organization had been in existence since March, 1849, under the name of the North street M. E. church of Rochester.

Another appropriation was made to aid in erecting what is the Alexander street church, on the corner of Alexander and Cobb streets, which was dedicated in the autumn of 1853, by Bishop E. S. Janes, D.D.

The Cornhill church was organized June 8, 1852, the above fund aiding essentially toward erecting the edifice that stands on Edinburgh street, near Plymouth avenue.

The Sixth M. E. church was organized December 17, 1852, under the impulse and practical encouragement derived from Mr. Champion's munificent gift. Its place of worship, on the corner of Smith and Frank streets, was dedicated in 1853, by Rev. J. S. Peck, D.D.

N. B.—It should be understood that while the noble

benefaction of Mr. Champion called some of these churches into being, and was of admitted importance in the way of encouragement, the amount in each case was but a small proportion of what was required to complete the structure.

NAMES OF METHODIST MINISTERS WHO HAVE BEEN STATIONED IN ROCHESTER.

Reverend Messrs.

Orren Miller, Cyrus Story,
Reuben Aylesworth, Elisha House,
Mica Seager, Isaac Puffer,
John Dempster, Zechariah Paddock,
Gideon Lanning, Gleason Fillmore,
Robert Burch, Elijah Hebard,
John Copeland, Allen Steele,
Daniel P. Kidder, D.D., Wilbur Hoag,
Jonas Dodge, Thomas Carlton,
Moses Crow, Samuel Luckey, D.D.,
Schuyler Seager, D.D., John Dennis,
John G. Gulick, A. C. George,
Jonathan Watts, D. D. Buck, D.D.,
Israel H. Kellogg, John Parker,
William H. Goodwin, D.D., LL.D.,
Manly Tooker, J. M. Fuller,
W. W. Mandeville, John Raines,
Thomas Tousey, Thomas Stacey,
D. W. C. Huntington, D.D., James E. Latimer, D.D.,
F. G. Hibbard, D.D., Elijah Wood,
Henry VanBenschoten, E. J. Hermans,
D. Leisenring, A. H. Shurtleff,

M. Wheeler,
John N. Brown,
S. W. Alden,
R. Hogoboom,
Thomas B. Hudson,
S. VanBenschoten,
George W. Paddock,
Albert N. Fisher,
J. Ashworth,

Nathan Fellows,
Alpha Wight,
George W. Chandler,
William Manning,
S. L. Congdon,
S. B. Rooney,
W. B. Holt,
Isaac Gibbard,
George VanAlstyne.

While all have been men of devotion to their sacred calling, and had much success in "winning souls to Christ," several of them have occupied, and still hold, a large place in public esteem, for scholarship and official station in church and state. As illustrations:

Rev. Daniel P. Kidder, D.D., a graduate of Wesleyan university, Conn., went as a missionary to Brazil, S. A., where he resided three years; travelled extensively from San Paulo to the equator; distributed bibles and various christian books, and preached the first sermon on the waters of the Amazon. Returning to the United States he published two volumes, entitled "Sketches of residence in Brazil," and, conjointly with Rev. J. C. Fletcher, "Brazil and the Brazilians," both of them well received by the literary and religious public, doing much to awaken an interest which has embodied itself in the present successful missions to those distant and needy regions. As a preacher, scholar, and author, Dr. Kidder occupies a high position in public regard.

Rev. Freeborn G. Hibbard, D.D., is a native of New Rochelle, N. Y.; commenced public life at the early age of eighteen, and has repeatedly held the highest positions in the gift of his church associates. As editor of the Northern Christian Advocate, and author of "Baptism, its Import and Efficacy," "Geography and History of Palestine," and the "Psalms Chronologically Arranged," Dr. Hibbard has displayed, as in his pulpit discourses, a well disciplined mind, profound scholarship, and accurate acquaintance with Bible truths. As a preacher, he is always listened to with interest and profit.

Rev. Zachariah Paddock, D.D., was born in Montgomery county, N. Y. ; when licensed, was placed on the Ontario district ; was ordained by the late Bishop Roberts, at Vienna (now Phelps) ; has been in charge of most of the stations in central and western New York, among them Buffalo, Rochester, Ithaca, Auburn, Utica, &c. ; held the office of presiding elder eighteen years, and is now at Binghamton. Though not a college graduate, he was studious and a master of many literary departments, all which attainments he has used to good effect with pen and voice. Benevolent and genial, he has many ardent friends in central and western New York, where for nearly half a century he has been abundant in labors to build up Zion, and spread scriptural holiness through the land.

Rev. Gleason Fillmore was born in Bennington, Vt. In 1818 he is found preaching at Buffalo and Black Rock, multitudes thronging to hear him. The most remarkable years of his ministry were spent in Rochester, in 1830–1, when a revival occurred, which added nine hundred to the church in this region. His manly figure, powerful voice, and earnest utterances, made him a favorite preacher at camp meetings, executions, and other public gatherings. He now resides near Buffalo.

Rev. John Dempster, D.D., was born in Florida, Fulton county, N. Y., his father being a native of Scotland, and for a time a follower of Wesley, though at the time of his death of and in the Presbyterian church. The subject of this sketch was converted at a camp meeting, and thenceforth was devoted to Christ with unabated and intense zeal. A hard student in early life, he became a "master in Israel." Being admitted to the general conference in 1816, his circuit was a vast wilderness, with fatigues and perils innumerable. The places he served were Watertown, Scipio, Homer, Auburn, Rochester, &c., where his resistless logic and sweeping eloquence are well remembered by the pioneer dwellers. Failing in health he spent six years in Buenos Ayres, S. A., and in 1842 became pastor of a church in New York. A surgical operation terminated his life in November, 186–; "and his end was peace."

Rev. Samuel Luckey, D.D., was born in Renselaerville, N. Y., his first circuit being in Ottawa, Lower Canada, then at St. Francis, in the same province, subsequently in Easton, N. Y., and New England, then in and around Albany, Troy, Schenectady, &c. For four years he was principal of Genesee seminary at Lima, and then editor of the Christian Advocate, at New York. Returning to itineracy, we find him in the metropolis, then on the Genesee conference, where he remained till his death in Rochester city, October 11, 1869, being at the time of his decease chaplain of the city penitentiary. "His fame is in all the churches, standing unsullied by any exceptional event of a moral, doctrinal, or ecclesiastical aberration, during the rare ministerial period of fifty-eight years." He was a regent of the State university.

William Henry Goodwin, D.D., LL.D., is a native of Trumansburgh, N. Y.; was educated at Lima, and received scholastic degrees at Hobart college, Geneva, and Dickenson college, Penn. He has been an active pastor for twenty-seven years, and presiding elder for seven years. During the winter of 1855-6 Dr. Goodwin represented his district in the senate of New York State, returning to his home in Geneva each Sunday, and officiating on the Sabbath. During the second winter of the term he admitted one hundred to church membership on profession of their faith, travelling weekly six hundred miles, and not being once absent from his seat at the capital. In the year 1865 he was chosen regent of the State, and took a leading part in the late Methodist convocation at Syracuse. His published writings have been of rather a fugative character, the most important being a speech on the "naturalization laws," an oration at Lima in 1852, and on Decoration Day.

A vast German (Methodist) population, unused to any but their own language, are scattered all through the land. Though under the supervision of the Bishops of the Methodist church, they have a conference of their own, and are served by ministers of the German tongue. That in this city is entitled First German Methodist Episcopal church, and is located on the corner of North and Tyler streets. It was organized in 1848, and has had as its ministers : Revs. John Sawter, John J. Crau, Jacob Kindler, Charles Afflerbach, A. C. Hortel, F. G. Gratz (twice), C. Blunn, J. G. Lutz, J. Kolb, and Paul Quatlander.

Zion church (Methodist), now located on the corner of Spring and Favor streets, was organized in 1835, and has had a checquered career, though now prosperous. The pastors have been : Revs. Isaac Steward, the early founder ; Henry Johnson, deceased ; John P. Thompson, Dempsy Kennedy, William S. Bishop, bishop, now in Newark, N. J. ; John A. Williams, ——— Thomas, James H. Smith, William Sandford, William Abbott, and Thomas James, the present incumbent.

From this church there entered the ministry German Logan, now a bishop, and resides at Syracuse.

Another church was organized in 1867, under the pastoral charge of Rev. William Edwards. The trustees being Messrs. Austin Steward, Peter Stockton, George Washington, David Winer, and Benjamin Jointer. This has been disbanded and the house of worship sold.

Prominent among the people of color was Austin Steward, whose autobiography, entitled "Twenty-Two Years a Slave, and Forty a Freeman," published by William Alling, in 1867, is a volume of much interest and well entitled to the recommendatory note signed by leading citizens, and a letter from ex-Governor Clark, of Canandaigua, and Edwin Scrantom, Esq., of this city. Mr. Steward was a man of much intellectual ability, great energy of character, and undaunted heroism in what he deemed the path of duty.

Whoever questioned his judgement, few, if any, doubted his honesty of aim. In mind, heart, and life, Mr. Steward was no common man.

Mr. John W. Bishop has a pleasant home on Adams street, where the writer spent a recent hour gathering the material for this brief but important chapter.

SUMMARY, JULY 1, 1871.

First—Rev. W. Loyd.
S. S. Superintendent—James Vick.

Asbury—Rev. F. G. Hibbard, D.D.
S. S. Superintendent—A. Manderville.

Cornhill—Rev. R. O. Wilson.
S. S. Superintendent—N. L. Button.

Alexander Street—Rev. J. D. Requa.
S. S. Superintendent—A. P. Ross.

North Street—Rev. J. N. Brown.
S. S. Superintendent—G. P. Davis.

First German—Rev. Paul Quatlander.
S. S. Superintendent—J. U. Flad.

Zion (Colored)—Rev. Thomas James.
S. S. Superintendent—John Weir.

Aggregate of Communicants—1,500.

BAPTIST.

FIRST CHURCH.

Previous to the year 1816, a few Baptists residing in the neighboring town of Brighton met in private houses for religious worship, under the leadership of Elders Drake and Lamb. Out of this company sprang an association which was formally organized in June, 1817, the place of gathering being a barn belonging to Deacon Graves, about three and a half miles from the present city. The members thus joined in covenant were Deacon Amos and Mrs. Anne Graves, Mr. Ira and Mrs. Sperry, Mr. Johnson and Mrs. Sperry, Mr. John and Mrs. Reynolds, Deacon Tenny, and Mrs. Urana M. Kennedy. The ministers assisting at this inauguration were Elders Lamb, Bramin, Brown, and Tinney, with Mr. Immer Reynolds as clerk. Such was the infancy of an ecclesiastical organization which now catalogues its hundreds of members, and has founded an University and a Theological seminary which reflect high honor upon the founders, are a credit to the city, and a blessing to the world.

Destitution of any place of worship seriously impeded early advancement, as it prevented many from joining the body who were one with them in doctrine, education, and early usage. The infant church at length engaged the services of Rev. E. M. Spencer, a teacher in Middlebury academy, "the eloqence of whose address awakened sanguine hopes that he would be extensively useful in the then rising village." Inability of support compelled him to resign in less than a year after settlement. He was succeeded, in 1823, by Rev. Eleazer Savage, during whose able and faithful ministry of three years the communicants increased from thirty-five to eighty-five in number. After the resignation of Mr. Savage, the prayers and labors of the laity were rewarded by seeing constant additions, so that when Rev. O. C. Comstock, M.D., came he found a people ready to coöperate in his zealous efforts for their spirituality, prosperity, and growth. After some delay and much pecuniary sacrifice, purchase was made of the edifice on Carroll (now State) street which the Presbyterians had left for their new home in rear of the court house. It was here that in 1831 the Lord so signally blest His truth that during twelve months one hundred and fifty were added by baptism and fifty-three by letter. Among the many whom Dr. Comstock had the privilege of welcoming to the Lord's table was a gifted son, who abandoned a promising career at the bar, devoted himself to theology, went to Burmah as a missionary, where he and his sainted wife lie buried on Pagan soil—a noble sacrifice upon the altar of Christ and souls. Upon the retirement of Dr. Comstock, through ill health, Rev. Pharcellus Church, D.D., took his place, during whose administration (in 1839) the edifice on North Fitzhugh street was built, which, though plain in outward appearance, holds an oftimes thronged assembly of worshipers. This is now giving place to another on the same site, to cost $125,000. The lecture room is now completing, and will be ready for occupancy before summer closes. The deacons, at the time of dedication, were Messrs. John Watts, Oren Sage, and John Jones; the trustees were Messrs. E. F. Smith, John Jones, John Watts, Oren Sage, and Charles Smith, with Mr. H. B. Sherman as clerk. Messrs. A. G. Smith, H. L. Achilles, Myron Strong, Edwin Pancost, George Davison, Charles Hubbell, and Ellery S. Treat have held important offices. Succeeding Dr. Church were Rev. Justin A. Smith (1849—1853), Rev. Jacob R. Scott (1855—1858), Rev. Richard M. Scott (1859), and the present incumbent.

PASTORS.

Rev. Eleazer Savage, a native of Middletown, Conn., and graduate of Hamilton Literary and Theological seminary, became the first settled pastor of the Baptist church in Rochester in the year 1823, and resigned after a short time to become pastor at Medina, Oswego, Albion, Holley, York, and Bath. He now resides at Fairport, spending the last days of a long and useful career on earth, his ministry having ever been earnest, faithful, and replete with blessed results.

Rev. Oliver C. Comstock, M.D., was a native of Rhode Island, and son of the late Hon. Adam Comstock, of Saratoga, a jurist of eminent ability and large repute. His education was limited to the common school and home. The University of New York having conferred upon him the degree of M.D., he practiced medicine for eight years at Trumansburgh; was appointed first judge of Seneca county, then State legislator, and Congressman for three terms, declining a fourth nomination that he might enter the ministry. He was ordained at Washington, D. C.; ministered at Ulysses and Ithaca; became pastor of the First Baptist church in this city in 1827, where he remained till May, 1835, when he resigned; was elected chaplain of the House of Representatives, and then removed to Marshall, Mich., where he held several positions of public trust and honor. The closing days of his long, eventful, and useful life were spent under the roof of his son, M. C. Comstock, M.D., going to his heavenly rest at the advanced age of seventy-nine. An obituary notice, taken from a Marshall journal, commences thus: "A truly great and good man has fallen." It was remarked by one who knew him well that "Dr. Comstock never had an enemy." "The memory of the just is blessed."

Rev. Pharcellus Church, D.D., was born in Seneca, near Geneva, Ontario county, N. Y., and commenced his ministry in Vermont, passing thence to Providence, R. I., being then transferred to New Orleans, from whence he came to Rochester in September, 1835, and resigned after an able and successful pastorate of the First Baptist church for thirteen years. During this period nearly one thousand persons were added to the church by baptism and letter. In 1848 Dr. Church removed to Boston and took charge of the Bowdoin Baptist church, which ill health compelled him to resign, and from 1855 to '65 he edited the Chronicle, of New York. Dr. Church has been a voluminous and popular author. Among his published works are "Philosophy of Benevolence," "Religious Dissensions," "Antioch," "Pentecost," with a multitude of pamphlets, etc. While here he interested himself much and practically in organizing the University, though leaving before he was privileged to see the results of his arduous and self-sacrificing labors in that direction.

Rev. Justin A. Smith, D.D., is a native of Ticonderoga, N. Y., and graduate of Union college, Schenectady. His pastorate of the First Baptist church began in the autumn of 1849, and continued four years, when he removed to Chicago, Ill., and became editor of the Christian Times, now styled the Standard, the denominational organ for the north-west, which he has conducted these eighteen years with marked ability and success. Associated with his editorial labors has been the charge of a city church, making his life one of labor and responsibility, but of extensive influence and much usefulness.

Rev. Jacob R. Scott, a native of Massachusetts; graduated at Brown university and Newton Theological seminary; was settled at Petersburgh, Va., from whence he came to Rochester in 1855, and remained three years, when he removed to Yonkers, N. Y., where he died.

Rev. Richard M. Nott was born in Nashua, N. H.; graduated at Colby university, Maine; was ordained pastor of First Baptist church, Rochester, October 12, 1859; resigned October, 1865; settled in Aurora, Ill., in 1869, where he now resides.

Rev. Henry E. Robins, D.D., was born in Hartford,

Conn.; graduated at Newton Theological seminary; ministered to a church at Newport, R. I.; came to this city, and was installed pastor of the First Baptist church in 1867.

MINISTERS AND MISSIONARIES FROM THIS CHURCH.

Rev. Zenas Freeman, deceased.
Rev. Grover S. Comstock, missionary to Burmah, deceased.
Rev. Joshua Ambrose, Michigan.
Rev. Niles Kinne, Wisconsin.
Rev. J. W. Spoor, New York city.
Rev. Stephen W. Tower, New Jersey.
Rev. Augustus H. Strong, D.D., Cleveland, Ohio.
Rev. Robert J. McArthur, New York.
Rev. Ezra Zeburn, Rochester.
Rev. William L. Lisle, Massachusetts.

SUMMARY, JULY 1, 1871.

Pastor—Rev. Henry E. Robins, D.D.
Deacons—Messrs. E. F. Smith, H. N. Langworthy, Alvah Strong, William N. Sage, L. R. Satterlee, Alfred G. Mudge, S. A. Ellis, J. O. Pettengill, and Austin H. Cole.
Clerk—Henry W. Dean.
Assistant Clerk—Henry S. Dean.
S. S. Superintendent—S. A. Ellis, with assistants A. R. Pritchard and E. R. Andrews.
Secretary and Treasurer—A. S. Lane.

Librarians—Henry S. Dean and W. Lincoln Sage.
Scholars—475.
Communicants—712.

OUT-STATIONS.

In connection with the First Baptist church is the Memorial Baptist Mission chapel, located on Lake avenue. This was commenced as a mission chapel in 1865, and became a distinct and separate organization in March, 1871, with one hundred and two members. The Sabbath school contains four hundred scholars, under the superintendence of Mr. D. A. Woodbury. The deacons are Messrs. Edwin Waite, D. A. Woodbury, and S. Glass.

Also, St. Paul street Mission, established in 1868, having a Sabbath school with three hundred scholars and three teachers.

Also, stations at Hanford's Landing, hereafter to be conducted by the Lake avenue church; and one on the Lyle road.

SECOND CHURCH.

At the beginning of the year 1834, it became the settled conviction of many members of the First Baptist church, that a new organization was necessary to meet the wants of the rapidly enlarging territory and ever increasing population. Accordingly on the 26th of February, 1834, fifty-six (56) persons were dismissed, to form a new interest on the east side of the river. Of the founders there are now living and in fellowship, David R. and Sarah M. Barton, Emeline Sheik, and Lydia A. Evans.

The Third Presbyterian church edifice, located on the corner of Main and Clinton streets, being then in market, was purchased, and the organization perfected on the 12th of May, 1834, under the title of the Second Baptist church of Rochester. The occasion was deepened in interest by the fact that on the day of organization Grover S. Comstock (son of the late Rev. O. Comstock, D.D.) was ordained a missionary to Burmah, whither he and his devoted wife went, never to return to their native country; and Zenas Freeman was set apart to the work of an evangelist.

On the night of December 10, 1859, this house of worship was consumed by fire, but another erected on

North street, near Main, during the year 1861, at an expense of $40,000, and far superior for size, commodiousness, and commanding attractions. This church has been ably ministered to by the following

PASTORS.

Rev. Elon Galusha, of Hamilton, N. Y., whose very acceptable services covered three years, when he resigned to become financial officer of Brockport college. He died at Brockport, January 4, 1856.

Rev. Elisha Tucker was installed January 1, 1837, and under his faithful ministry a revival occurred which added fifty persons to the communion. He resigned in 1841, removed to New York city, and died in 1853.

Rev. V. R. Hotchkiss became pastor April 26, 1842, and before the close of the year a revival resulted in the conversion of one hundred and forty-three persons (eighty-three of whom were from the Sunday school). In 1845 he resigned, and is now pastor of Washington street church, Buffalo.

Rev. Charles Thompson came in 1846 and left in less than a year, to become pastor of the Tabernacle church, which had a brief existence on St. Paul street. He is now pastor in Fredonia.

Rev. Henry Davis remained but a year and went to another field, leaving behind "the blessings of the poor and sorrowing for his kind attentions, and the gratitude of the church and community for the urbanity of his manners, and devotion to his calling."

Rev. W. G. Howard, D.D., commenced his labors

in the autumn of 1851, and was much blest in leading many to Christ. After a pastorate of six years he moved to Chicago, and then to New Orleans, where he died in 1863.

Rev. George Dana Boardman, D.D., is a native of Tavany Burma. His parents, the late Rev. George Dana Boardman and Sarah Hall (subsequently Mrs. Judson), occupy a prominent place on the page of modern foreign missions. Graduating at Brown university, R. I., and Newton Theological seminary, Mass., he passed a brief period at Barnwell Court House, S. C., when he assumed pastoral charge of this church October, 1856, occupying the same for eight years, when he left to preside over the First Baptist church of Philadelphia. In the departure of Dr. Boardman, Rochester lost a preacher, lecturer, and citizen of prominent ability and repute. Long will he be remembered for peculiar fascination as an orator, and varied acquirements as a public teacher.

Rev. J. H. Gilmore was installed October 1, 1865, but resigned after three years to take the chair of the Theological seminary in the city university.

Rev. T. Edwin Brown, of Brooklyn, commenced his labors November 1, 1869, which he meets with an ability and acceptance not at all behind his able predecessors.

If ever a church and parish had cause for gratitude to God for well qualified religious guides, this has in the persons of the nine who have stood, trumpet in hand, upon the walls of this part of the christian zion. The fifty-six who constituted the original membership have arisen to five hundred, deducting deaths and removals.

SUMMARY, JULY 1, 1871.

Pastor—Rev. L. Edwin Brown.

Deacons—Messrs. D. R. Barton, Thomas Johnson, A. Moseley, M. G. Seely, and William Richardson.

S. S. Superintendent—Mr. George W. Rawson, Mrs. Adolphus Morse.

No. of Teachers—51.

No. of Scholars—600.

Trustees—Messrs. John M. French, George Brown, C. B. Woodworth, E. D. Tracy, D. R. Barton, and Charles H. Williams.

No. of Communicants—570.

GERMAN CHURCH.

In 1848-9 several German Baptists came from New York and other places to this city, when they commenced holding meetings by themselves in private dwellings and in school house number ten, on Fitzhugh street. Their services were conducted first by Mr. G. Englehard, a colporteur of the American Tract society, and afterwards by Rev. C. Boos, of Warrensville, Penn., who labored here nine months, and Rev. J. Eschman, of New York, who spent a few weeks, and by others at different intervals, and for less periods of time.

In October, 1850, Mr. Henry Henrich came to the city from Buffalo, and because of his efficiency and success in collecting and cementing these scattered elements, may be styled the founder of the present organization, the German Baptist church. On the 29th of June, 1851, the body was regularly organized, and recognized by the related judicatories, Rev. Mr. Henrich being ordained as first pastor. Among the constituent members were Messrs. John Doppler, Jacob Bopser, Conrad Leppler, and Joseph Richard. During the pastorate of Rev. Mr. Henrich, many persons were added to the church by baptism and letter, a large portion of whom migrated from time to time to the west, several being excluded from fellowship through unfaithfulness to their covenant obligations. In October, 1858, Rev. Mr. Henrich removed to Anthony, Lycoming county, Pa. Rev. Prof. A. Rauschenbusch, of the Rochester Theological seminary, supplying the pulpit for about six months, when Rev. Gerhard Koopman was pastor for a brief time, who was succeeded, in 1863, by Rev. Henry Schneider, and he, in 1865, by Rev. Henry Tschirch, the present occupant.

When the church was first organized, services were held in a hall on Ann street, near State. After a few years purchase was made of school house number ten, on Andrews street, which is now taking down and an edifice of brick erecting, to cost about $8,000.

This church is ecclesiastically connected with the Monroe Baptist Association. The German students at the Theological seminary (generally about twelve in number), worship here, and render valuable aid in social meetings and in Sabbath schools.

SUMMARY, JULY 1, 1871.

Pastor—Rev. Earnest Tschirch.

Deacons—Messrs. Jacob Widmer, Joseph Richard, and George Guenther.

S. S. Superintendent—Alexander Trzeciak.

No. of Scholars—100.

Communicants—86.

CONGREGATIONAL.

FIRST CHURCH.

This organization was perfected about the year 1842, and that not so much on ecclesiastical grounds and from preference to the New England form of faith or worship, as from a warm sympathy of its founders in the anti-slavery movements of the times and with the acceptance by them of the doctrinal views upon sanctification, taught at Oberlin, Ohio. As the doctrine of christian perfection, and the ardent espousal of the anti-slavery cause, were the immediate occasion of constituting the church, so they were its characteristic features from commencement to dissolution.

The first minister was Rev. A. S. Shaffer, from New Jersey, who remained between two and three years, when Rev. Henry E. Peck (son of Everard Peck, Esq.) became the ordained pastor, and so continued for nearly eight years.

The church edifice was in the northern part of the city known as Frankfort, and the society was in a large measure composed of the inhabitants in that vicinity, with a few other earnest men and women, who sympathized with Oberlin views upon slavery and questions of theology.

In progress of time, when abolitionism came to be

tolerated in the churches, and Oberlinism had ceased to be treated as a dangerous heresy, and as a Methodist church had just been organized in the same suburbs of the city, there seemed no longer a special call for this organization to raise the cry in the wilderness, and, the Rev. Mr. Peck having been called to a professorship in Oberlin college, the church and society about the year 1851 was dissolved, and the members were quietly mixed with the other evangelical churches of the city.

The membership was about one hundred and twenty. Leonard Hitchcock and Joseph Higgins were the two deacons, and were both of the "salt of the earth," and have gone to their reward above. The church served its intended purpose — its career, though brief, being greatly useful and honored.

FREE CHURCH.

Was organized in November, 1836, with five members, which soon increased to seventy. The first pastor was Rev. John T. Avery, and trustees were Messrs. John Gorton and Willis Sterns. A place of worship was erected on the corner of St. Paul and Division streets, between Main street and Saint Paul church.

PLYMOUTH CHURCH.

September 8, 1853, saw laid the corner-stone of Plymouth church, on the corner of Troup and Sophia streets, now called Plymouth avenue. The occasion called together a large concourse of citizens; Presbyterian, Methodist, and Baptist clergymen taking part in the interesting exercises. Rev. O. E. Daggett, D.D., then of Canandaigua, delivered an appropriate address. The funds needful for the construction of the massive building were largely contributed by Aristarchus Champion, Esq., who, after its completion, conveyed the property by deed to the trustees, August 10, 1855. An act of State incorporation was obtained, under date of April 15, 1854, and the following persons were elected trustees: Messrs. Aristarchus Champion, Freeman Clarke, Edmund Lyon, Charles J. Hill, William W. Ely, M.D., A. G. Bristol, M.D., E. H. Hollister, C. A. Burr, and Erastus Darrow.

An ecclesiastical organization was perfected August 21, 1855, with seventy members, of whom Ezra B. Booth, Eliza A. Bloss, Robert E. Brewster, Dr. A. G. and Mrs. Mary G. Bristol, Aristarchus Champion, Erastus Darrow, Olivia H. Dewey, Dr. L. C. and Mrs. Sarah Dolley, Dr. W. W. and Mrs. Sarah and Angeline Ely, Joseph Farley, Dennis Hartwell, Elizabeth Lee, Alice B. Peck, Galusha and Stella B. Phillipps, Samuel C. and Susan F. Porter, Smith R. and Lucy A. Sutherland, William H. and Sarah B. Thomas, Frederick, Matilda and Frank VanDoorn, Porter W. and Emeline C. Taylor are still in communion.

On the evening of the same day the church edifice was dedicated to the worship of God, the sermon being preached by Rev. Jonathan Edwards, of Woburn, Mass., and devotional exercises conducted by Rev. Drs. Daggett, of Canandaigua, Leonard Bacon, of New Haven, Joseph P. Thompson, of New York, with Rev. Messrs. J. H. Dill, E. W. Gilman, and T. Eddy. At a church meeting held December 10, 1855, Rev. Jonathan Edwards was unanimously elected pastor, and was installed April 18, 1856; the sermon being preached by Rev. Prof. Parks, of Andover (Mass.) Theological seminary. Ill health compelled a resignation November 2, 1862. Mr. Edwards returned to his native State, leaving behind universal esteem as a gentleman of intellectual culture, urbanity of manner, united with diligence, ability, and faithfulness as preacher and pastor. The pulpit was variously supplied till the unanimous call of the present incumbent, Rev. Dwight K. Bartlett, who was installed May 9, 1869.

PASTORS.

Rev. Jonathan Edwards, son of the late Justin Edwards, D.D., president of Andover Theological seminary, was born at Andover; graduated at Yale college and at Andover seminary; was first settled at

Woburn, Mass., from which place he came to Rochester, and was installed first pastor of Plymouth church in April, 1856, where he remained nearly seven years. He has now charge of the ancient church of Dedham, Mass., founded in the year 1636. During his pastorate in Rochester two hundred and forty persons united with the church.

Rev. Dwight K. Bartlett was born in Poughkeepsie; graduated at Union college and Princeton and Union Theological seminaries; preached at Amenia, N. Y., and Stamford, Conn.; coming to Rochester in 1859, where he labors among an attached people.

In connection with the pastors of Plymouth church, mention may be made of another person, who, though never holding an official position, was so often in the pulpit, and so thoroughly identified with this body and with religion, science, and education throughout the city, as to merit special and emphatic record.

Rev. Charles Dewey, D.D., LL.D., was born at Sheffield, Mass.; graduated at Williams college, of which institution he was an officer for seventeen years. During the next ten years he was president of the Gymnasium at Pittsfield, Mass., when, in 1836, he came to this city as principal of the Rochester Collegiate Institute, located where now stands the Third Presbyterian church, on the east side of the river, and where many of our leading citizens received their early education, and live to retain a grateful memory of their accomplished and revered teacher. In the year 18— Dr. Dewey assumed the chair of Chemistry and Natural Philosophy in the then newly established University of Rochester, which he held with well known repute for ten years, when he resigned its active duties, though still retained as Emeritus Professor. As a gentleman, a scholar, a teacher, a writer, and christian divine, Dr. Dewey was extensively known and universally esteemed. When, on the 15th of December, 1867, he expired, at his residence on Troup street, it was felt that Rochester had lost a gifted resident, science an acknowledged master, the church a warm-hearted disciple, and his home a cherished head.

SUMMARY, JULY 1, 1871.

Pastor—Rev. Dwight K. Bartlett.

Deacons—Messrs. S. D. Porter, H. M. McLean, P. W. Handy, and A. G. Bristol.

Trustees—Messrs. C. J. Hill, W. N. Emerson, Henry Brewster, Galusha Phillips, Erastus Darrow, W. W. Ely, M.D., B. H. Clark, S. B. Roby, O. L. Sheldon.

S. S. Superintendent—A. S. Hamilton.

Scholars—250.

Church Membership—300.

Plymouth church has a colony under the title of the Eighth Ward Mission chapel, on the corner of Reynolds and Tremont streets. It was organized as a Sabbath school in February, 1867. At the present time it has two hundred and fifty scholars, with thirty-two teachers, under the superintendency of Mr. William B. Levet. Cottage prayer and Bible reading meetings are held every Friday evening. An useful future is in hopeful prospect.

SINGLE CHURCHES.

ZION'S FIRST EVANGELICAL LUTHERAN CHURCH.

This religious community was organized with twenty members, in the year 1834, in a frame house on Pioneer street. A lot on the corner of Grove and Stillson streets being donated for that purpose, a spacious brick edifice was erected, and is the present place of worship.

The Pastors have been: Rev. John Muehlauser, deceased ; Rev. H. G. Kempie, deceased ; Rev. A. Uebelacker, studying medicine ; Rev. Fred. VonRosenberg, a native of Germany, and student of Berlin, Erlanger and Bunn, who came to this country in 1863, and was installed pastor in 1868, which position he now holds with efficiency and usefulness.

SUMMARY, JULY 1, 1871.

Pastor—Rev. Fred. VonRosenberg.

Elders—Messrs. Phillip Meyer, John Bohr, and Julius Binder.

Deacons—Messrs. William Wagner, Peter Hartman, Henry Buhlmann, John Unglink, David Bartleon, Jacob Margrander, and Nicholas Conrad.

S. S. Superintendent—Jesse Shepherd, an elder of the Third Presbyterian church.

Scholars—450. *Communicants*—1,000.

GERMAN UNITED EVANGELICAL CHURCH.

Was organized in the year 1842. The first officers after the incorportion were Messrs. Lorens Raab, Bernhard Haid, and John G. Beck as trustees; Carl Rohrig, Henry A. Merlan, and Henry Lux, deacons; with Messrs. George G. Bachman, John Knodel, and Matthias Hertel as elders. The congregation met in public halls and rented rooms until 1847, when a church was built on Allen street, nearly opposite the Brick Presbyterian church, where services are still held.

PASTORS.

Rev. C. F. Solden, Rev. C. Biehl, deceased, Rev. Birke, Rev. Illiger, Rev. C. Haas, Rev. C. Clawson, Rev. J. H. Conradt.

SUMMARY, JULY 1, 1871.

Pastor—Rev. Charles Siebenpfeiffer.
Elders—Messrs. Adam Schake, Matthias Hertel, and L. Wehn.

Deacons—Messrs. F. Ruckdeschel, Joseph Fitzenberger, Wilhelm Heul, John Frick, and Franz Harwart.

S. S. Superinteddent—Mr. Thomas Dransfield.

Scholars—200.

Communicants—900.

There is a day school with two hundred scholars, under care of Messrs. John C. Gauger, C. Schopper, and Miss Augusta Kingsbury.

The parish contains four societies: one for benevolent and mutually benevolent purposes; another, consisting of married ladies, for relief of the poor; another, containing young ladies alone, for promoting church interests; and a fourth, young men alone, for for educating and cultivating young men.

FIRST GERMAN EVANGELICAL ASSOCIATION.

Located on St. Joseph, corner Nassau street (but formerly on Stillson street), was organized in 1848, by Rev. J. G. Marquardt, now in California. Previous to that time several ministers of the Evangelical Association, held services here, though irregularly and with little concentration of effort. As the ministers of this body cannot stay in one place more than two years, the following have been here as

PASTORS.

Revs. J. Wagner, J. Schaaf, M. Laner, L. Jacoby, A. Klenn, S. Weaver, A. Miller, P. J. Miller, G. Eckhard, A Hobswarth.

SUMMARY, JULY 1, 1871.

Pastor—Rev. Michael Lehn.

S. S. Superintendent—Rudolph Luescher.

Scholars—200.

Communicants—119.

FIRST ENGLISH LUTHERAN CHURCH.

Was organized July 18, 1869, under the ecclesiastical direction of the present pastor, Rev. Reuben Hill. This reverend gentlemen is a native of Pennsylvania, a graduate of Pennsylvania college, at Gettysburgh, where he preached for a time, and then at Hagerstown, Md., at Pittsburgh, Pa., coming here in December, 1868, where he has commenced an enterprise which is destined to assume large proportions and exert great power.

SUMMARY, JULY 1, 1871.

Pastor—Rev. Reuben Hill.
Elders—Messrs. C. M. Meyer, and Charles Schomaker.
Deacons—Messrs. Jacob Suter, Frederick Moser, and G. W. Arnold.
S. S. Superintendent—Jesse Shepherd.
Scholars—260.
Communicants—75.

Present place of worship, a room in a building on Grove, near North street. A church edifice will, it is hoped, ere long be erected for the use of this growing society.

EVANGELICAL REFORMED EMANUEL CHURCH.

Was organized in the year 1851; the edifice is located on Hamilton Place, in the 12th ward, near Mt. Hope; the pastor is Rev. Charles Kuss, who, after several years of missionary life in Russia, was settled here in the year 1869; the Sabbath school superintendent is Mr. Jacob Wentz.

EVANGELICAL SAINT PAUL'S CHURCH.

Was organized in 1864; the building is located on Fitzhugh street; the pastor is Rev. Frederick Heinle, who was settled in 1869; the Sunday school superintendent is Mr. C. A. Becker. This church is Lutheran in doctrine and form of government.

FIRST REFORMED (DUTCH) CHURCH.

This church, located on the corner of Oregon and Harrison streets, was organized in the year 1848. The founders were J. VanDoven, Levinus Verhagen, Abraham Eevnipe, and —— Kots; the presiding officer being Rev. S. Bolks, of the classis of Holland, Mich.

The pastors have been: Rev. A. B. Veerhauzen, now at East Williamson, N. Y.; Rev. W. C. Wurt, now at Lodi, N. Y.; Rev. A. Krickaart, now at Kalamazoo, Mich.; Rev. Pierre B. Bähler, the present pastor, was born at Twolle, Netherlands, where his father had ministered for over forty years. After a course of education by his parent, he preached in Belgium, and was one of the founders of the Belgium Evangelical Society. Returning to the Netherlands, he remained in charge of two churches till he came to this country, October 15, 1869. At a brief sojourn and ministrations at Albany, N. Y., and Paterson, N. J., he came to this city in March, 1868, and is earnestly engaged in organizing his countrymen and leading them in the course of truth and heaven.

There is a Sabbath school of fifty-six pupils, under the superintendency of the pastor. The communicants are 231. The church belongs to the classis of Geneva, and is Dutch Reformed in its policy.

FIRST UNIVERSALIST CHURCH.

While Rochester was but a village, followers of this theological faith were accustomed to meet for worship in the school house and the court room, the preachers being Rev. —— Sampson, Rev. Henry Roberts (father of George H. Roberts, Esq.), Rev. William Andrews, Rev. Jacob Chase, Rev. T. B. Abel, Rev. Russell Tomlinson, and Rev. Charles Hammond. They then worshiped in the Court street church, until it was sold to the Scotch Presbyterians. Being without a place of worship, Sabbath school only was continued in the basement of the Unitarian church on Fitzhugh street, till the arrival of Rev. Mr. Montgomery, when they resumed services in Minerva hall, and continued until the erection of a plain structure on Chestnut, near Main street, which has been recently enlarged and beautified at great expense, being re-dedicated March 22, 1871 — the discourse being preached by Rev. Dr. Saxe, and devotional services by Rev. Messrs. Montgomery, Mann, and other clergymen.

Among the founders and early members of this church were Messrs. Joseph Wood, deceased; Isaac Hellums, —— Gilman; Schuyler Moses, John Baxter, John B. Beers, M.D., J. J. VanZandt, J. F. Boyce, and N. Bingham.

PASTORS.

Rev. George Montgomery, a native of Portland, Maine, was installed December, 1845, and served eight years, when ill health compelled his resignation. He is a resident of the city, greatly respected by all who know him.

Rev. J. W. Tuttle held the position for about six years, and was succeeded by

Rev. A. Saxe, D.D., the present scholarly and popular incumbent, under whose pastorate the church is greatly prospering.

YOUNG MEN WHO HAVE ENTERED THE MINISTRY.

Rev. Stephen R. Camp, now at Brooklyn.
Rev. William Vandemark, now at Pittsburgh, Pa.
Rev. J. Murray Bailey, now at Titusville, Pa.
Edwin S. Corbin, in the Theological seminary.

SUMMARY, JULY 1, 1871.

Pastor—Rev. Asa Saxe, D.D.
Deacons—Messrs A. C. Wilmot and George H. Roberts.
S. S. Superintendent—W. E. Cooke.
Scholars—200.
Communicants—About 100.

NOTE.—The society inaugurated the now popular custom of Sunday school railroad excursions.

FIRST UNITARIAN CONGREGATIONAL SOCIETY.

This ecclesiastical body was formally organized July 18, 1841. An edifice erected on North Fitzhugh street in 1842–3, was destroyed by fire, November 10, 1859, in consequence of which regular services were suspended till 1865, when the corner stone of the present sanctuary, opposite the former, was laid with usual ceremonies, and the house dedicated in 1866.

Pastors in succession have been: Rev. J. P. B. Storer, D.D., deceased; Rev. F. A. Whitney, deceased; Rev. Rufus Dillis, Rev. Frederick W. Holland, Rev. —— Bacon, deceased; Rev. W. Dougherty, Rev. W. H. Channing, Rev. James Richardson, deceased; Rev. F. W. Holland, D.D., a second time, during whose pastorate the present structure was built in 1868; Rev. Clay McCauley, Rev. N. M. Mann.

SUMMARY, JULY 1, 1871.

Pastor—Rev. Newton M. Mann.
Deacon—John G. Williams.
Trustees—Messrs. J. L. Angle, Joseph Curtis, and Simon L. Brewster.
S. S. Superintendent—J. L. Angle.
Pupils—80. *Communicants*—50.

ROMAN CATHOLIC CHURCHES.

The first Roman Catholic congregation built a stone edifice in 1823, on Platt street, near State, the site of the present Saint Patrick's cathedral. Several clergymen had charge of the enterprise, conspicious among whom was Bernard O'Reilly, D.D., who was consecrated Roman Catholic Bishop of Connecticut in 1850, and was lost at sea in 1856.

It being quite impossible to present a detailed narrative of each separate organization of this large ecclesiastical body, it must suffice to append the following names and localities of churches, with the officiating officers, and various religious institutions in charge.

1. Saint Patrick's Cathedral; located on Platt street; founded in 1822; officiating clergy, Rev. B. J. McQuaid, D.D., bishop of diocese of Rochester, assisted by Rev. Messrs. J. M. Early, J. F. O'Hare, Nicholas Byrne, and H. D. Regge.

2. Saint Mary's church; South, near Court street; founded in 1842; officiating ministers, Rev. John Stewart, and James Mooney.

3. Saint Peter and Saint Paul's church; Maple street, corner King; founded in 1843; officiating minister, Rev. Francis H. Sinclair.

4. Saint Joseph's church, German; Franklin street; founded in 1846; officiating ministers, Rev. George Ruland, Peter Croneberg, Joseph Clauss, George Rorsch, A. Pingel, and Phillip Colonel.

5. Our Lday of Victory, French; Pleasant street; founded 1848; officiating minister, Rev. Joseph Dole.

6. Church Immaculate Conception; Plymouth Avenue; founded 1848; officiating minister, Rev. Patricio Byrnes.

7. Saint Bridget's church; Hand street; founded in 1854; officiating minister ——

8. Saint Bonifacius church, German; Grand street; founded in 1861; officiating minister, Rev. John Flor Payer.

9. Holy Redeemer's church; Hudson street, corner Clifford; officiating minister, Rev. Fidelis Oberholter.

RELIGIOUS SOCIETIES IN CITY UNDER BISHOP M'QUAID.

1. House of Redemptorists; adjoining Saint Joseph's church; Rev. George Ruland, rector.

2. Brothers of Mary; Franklin street.

3. School Sisters of Notre Dame; Andrews street.

4. Convent and Academy of the Sacred Heart; Madame Barratty, superior.

5. Convent and Academy of Our Lady of Mercy; Mother M. C. Kelley, superior.

6. Saint Mary's Hospital.

7. Saint Mary's Boy's Orphan Asylum.

8. Saint Patrick's Girl's Orphan Asylum.

9. Saint Joseph's Orphan Asylum, German.

Ten schools, containing 1,448 boys, and 1,513 girls; a large proportion are taught gratuitously.

FRIENDS NO. 1 — FRIENDS NO. 2.

A society of Friends was formed in 1817, and a meeting house was erected on Fitzhugh street, opposite the Brick church. In consequence of discussions, in which the name of Elias Hicks was frequently menioned, another society was formed in 1828, called the Orthodox Friends, who erected a place of worship on Jay street, in a part of the city called Frankfort. The trustees of this latter society were Messrs. Jesse Evans, Silas Cornel, and L. Atwater. Of the former: Messrs. Samuel Post and Joseph Green. So writes Henry O'Reilly, Esq., in his "Rochester and Western New York," under date of 1838.

SUMMARY, JULY 1, 1871.

Friends meeting house, Hubbell Park. No names of officers given in the Directory.

Friends meeting house, Jay street near Kent.

Pastor—Jacob D. Bell.

S. S. Superintendent—Mr. Lindley M. Murray.

Mr. Lindley M. Moore — father of our distinguished townsman, Edward M. Moore, M. D. — has just deceased. In his death the society of Friends lost a devoted and representative member; the oppressed a warm advocate; community a most worthy citizen, and a home a cherished parent and kinsman.

BERITH KODESH — AITZ RAH NON.

These are the names of the two Jewish congregations, the former,

Berith Kodesh, founded in 1843, is located on North St. Paul street, having both as pastor and Sunday school superintendent, Max Lansberg.

Aitz Rah Non, founded in 1870, and is located on St. Joseph street, with —— Rundbaken as pastor.

Connected with these congregations are the following benevolent societies:

1. Hebrew Benevolent Society; organized 1850; president, Henry Garson; secretary, Joseph Kauffman.

2. Ladies' Hebrew Benevolent Society; organized 1865; president, Mrs. A. Mock; secretary, Mrs. H. Britenstool.

SECOND ADVENT.

Organized 1867; place of worship, Washington Hall.

YOUNG MEN

ROCHESTER YOUNG MEN AND THE CHRISTIAN MINISTRY.

NATIVES OF ROCHESTER, AND THOSE COMING HERE VERY EARLY IN LIFE, WHO ENTERED THE MINISTRY AND BECAME PASTORS OR FOREIGN MISSIONARIES.

Names—Parentage—Church Connection—Residences—Alphabetically Arranged.

Bush, Charles P., D.D.—David Bush; Pres.; Norwich, Conn., Beloit, Wis., Rochester, Dist. Sec. A. B. C. F. M. at New York.

Bush, George C.—David Bush; Pres.; Stewarts and Hackelstown, N. J., Newton, Pa.

Bush, James S.—O. N. Bush; Ep.; San Francisco.

Bishop, George S.—W. S. Bishop; Pres.; N. Brunswick, N. J., Newburgh, N. Y.

Benedict, Wayland R.—Nehemiah W.; Bap.; Rochester.

Carpenter, Elisha M.—Cyril Carpenter; Pres.; Rochester and New York city.

Cherry, Henry—Pres.; missionary at S. India; died at the south.

Copeland, Jonathan—David Copeland; Pres.; Holley, N. Y., now in Vermont.

Clarke, Charles Russell—Charles L. Clarke; Pres.; Prof. in Princeton Coll., N. J., San Francisco, San Diego.
Chapin, Henry B., Ph.D.—Moses Chapin; Pres.; Steubenville, O., Trenton, N. J., New York city.
Comstock, Grover S.—Rev. O. Comstock; Bap.; foreign missionary in Burma, and died there.
Ely, Joseph A.—W. W. Ely, M.D.; Cong.; Rochester.
Gaylord, Willis S.—W. M. Gaylord; Pres.; Union Corners, Ossian, and Arkport, N. Y.
Green, Jonathan S.—Pres.; missionary to the Sandwich Islands.
Hall, Augustus F.—bro. of A. G. Hall, D.D.; Pres.; deceased.
Hamilton, Gavin L.—Pres.; Pittsford, Rochester.
Hall, Alanson C.—Pres.; missionary in India; died at the south.
Hunt, T. Dwight—Simeon Hunt, M.D.; Pres.; Sandwich Islands, Ithaca and Waterville, N. Y., Niles, Mich., San Francisco.
Hastings, Parsons C.—Orlando Hastings; Pres.; merchant in New York.
Jervis, Kasimir Pulaski—Asahal Hatch Jervis; Meth.; after serving in seven places, he is Presiding Elder of East Genesee Conference.
Johnson, Thomas H.—Pres.; Bricksburgh, N. J.
Kempshall, Everard, D.D.—Thos. Kempshall; Pres.; Buffalo and Batavia, N. Y., Elizabeth, N. J.
Lee, Charles G.—Charles M. Lee; Pres.; Syracuse, N. Y., died in Rochester.
Miller, L. Merrill, D.D.—Lewis Miller; Pres.; Bath and Ogdensburgh, N. Y.

Miller, Enoch—Pres.; army chaplain.

Pierpont, James S.—Rev. Hezekiah B. Pierpont; Ep.

Peck, Henry E.—Everard Peck; Pres.; Rochester, Prof. at Oberlin College, Consul General at Hayti, where he died in 1867.

Smith, L. Ward—S. O. Smith; Ep.; Albion, N. Y., Germantown, Pa., (1) rector St. Michael's, (2) Hospital Chaplain, where he died.

Shaw, Augustus C.—Rev. J. B. Shaw, D.D.; Pres.; Fulton, N. Y.

Starr, Frederick, Jr.—Frederick Starr; Pres.; Weston, Mo., Penn Yan, N. Y., St. Louis, Mo., where died in 1867.

Strong, Augustus H., D.D.—Alvah Strong; Baptist; Cleveland, Ohio.

Ward, George Kemp—L. A. Ward; Pres.; licentiate.

Ward, F. DeW., D.D.—L. Ward, M.D.; Pres.; missionary in S. India, Geneseo, chaplain in the army during the war.

Winslow, Horace—Pres.; Lansingburgh, N.Y., Rockville and New Britain, Conn., Great Barrington, Mass., Williamantic, Conn.

Witherspoon, Orlando W.—Samuel Witherspoon; Ep.; Buffalo.

Warren, Daniel F., D.D.—Ep.; New York city.

NOTE.—This list, though long, is, we fear, not complete. Names are not upon church records, and are lost to memory, which belong to this catalogue. Omissions, if any, were beyond the author's power to remedy. Should a second edition ever appear, this deficiency, and others, can be supplied.

MISCELLANY.

MISCELLANY.

LITERARY AND ECCLESIASTICAL PREFERMENTS OF ROCHESTER PASTORS.

Rev. Dr. Penny, Pres., Prest. of Hamilton Coll., N. Y.
Rev. Dr. Whitehouse, Ep., Bishopric of Illinois.
Rev. Dr. Lee, Ep., Bishopric of Iowa.
Rev. Dr. Neely, Ep., Bishopric of Maine.
Rev. Dr. O'Reilly, R. C., Bishopric of Connecticut.
Rev. Mr. Logan, Meth., Bishop at Syracuse.
Rev. Mr. Bishop, Meth., Bishop at New Jersey.
Rev. Dr. Patterson, Bap., Prest. of Waterville Coll.
Rev. Dr. Mack, Pres., Prest. of Tennessee Coll.
Rev. Dr. Colton, Ep., Prest. Bristol Coll.
Rev. Dr. VanRensellaer, Ep., Prest. DeVeaux Coll.
Rev. Dr. Edwards, Pres., Prest. of Wilson Coll.
Rev. Dr. Morgan, Pres., Prest. of a Southern Coll.
Rev. Dr. Parker, Pres., Prest. Union Theol. Sem.
Rev. Dr. McIlvaine, Pres., Prof. in Princeton Coll.
Rev. Dr. Claxton, Ep., Prof. in Phila. Theol. Sem.
Rev. Dr. Wm. Wisner, Pres., Mod. G. A. in 1840.
Rev. Dr. W. C. Wisner, Pres., Mod. G. A. in 1855.
Rev. Dr. Shaw, Pres., Mod. G. A. in 1863.
Rev. Dr. Comstock, Bap., Chaplaincy of Congress.
Rev. Dr. Luckey, Meth., Regent of the State of N. Y.
Rev. Dr. Goodwin, Meth., Regent of the State of N. Y.

In addition to these are the names of
Rev. Dr. Pease, Pres., Ex-Prest. of the Univ. of Vt.
Rev. Dr. Yeomans, Pres., Trans'r of Lange's Com.
Rev. Dr. Kendrick, Bap., Trans'r of Olshausen, &c.
Rev. Dr. Dewey, Con., Christian Scientist and Author.
Rev. Mr. Morris, Pres., Author of "Bible and Nature."
Rev. Drs. Church, Cheeseman, Bush, McIlvaine, Wisner (W. C.), Luckey, Hibbard, Ward, Authors.

LONG PASTORATES.

It is rare to meet in our day and land instances parrallel to those of Drs. Hall and Shaw, of the Third and Brick churches, each for more than thirty years pastor of the same society. The two united terms carry us back to a period when this region was unsettled but "by the wolf and the wild deer, or the red hunter, untutored and untamed as they." May these faithful and honored servants of God and the people long live to advance the truth as it is in Jesus.

Drs. Penny and Edwards were here each ten years, and Dr. Whitehouse fourteen.

DESIRABLE CHANGES OF USE.

The first theatre and the first circus in the "village" of Rochester were so unpopular as to prove pecuniary failures. After a brief career, the former, located on opposite Market street, was "converted" into a livery stable, and the latter, on the site of Aldrich's carpenter shop, into a soap chandlery and then into an iron foundry. In 1838, neither circus nor theatre existed here.—*O'Reilly's History, p. 117.*

REVIVALS.

Our pulpit occupants, from Drs. Penny, Wisner, Parker, Cumming, Whitehouse, Comstock, Fillmore, and Tucker, through a long line to the present able incumbents, did not "labor in vain and spend their strength for nought." The communion occasions that saw no additions were "few and far between." But it was left for those seasons when the Spirit came down "like rain upon the mown grass," to witness those ingatherings of souls which attracted hither the wondering eye of the nation, and evoked glad praises above. The writer, in common with many of his readers, remembers, among the events of early boyhood, the crowds that thronged the plain, unpainted school house which stood on the site of the Union school; the space being too limited to contain those who met to hear the truth and bow in penitence and prayer. In the year 1830, Rev. Charles G. Finney commenced preaching about the first of September, which he continued almost daily for six months. The place then contained ten thousand inhabitants, of whom eight hundred were hopefully converted during that memorable winter. Mr. Finney was again here in 1842, and again in 1856, with abundant and blessed results attending his plain, direct, earnest, bold declarations of divine truth. That great and good man, having survived all the associates of his middle life, is still serving his Master as pulpit preacher and as president of Oberlin college, Ohio. The late Rev. Jedediah Burchard was here in 1833, and again in 1842, addressing large assemblages with abundant immediate effects, though with much that was exceptionable in manner, and less that was permanently beneficial in result. While Mr. Finney addressed the intellect, Mr. Burchard appealed to the passions. The one was a masterly and bold logician; the other was the dramatic orator, holding wrapt attention, and swaying feelings at his will. Rev. E. P. Hammond visited the city in 1863 and in 1869, crowding the largest churches with auditors, especially the young. Strike from the roll of membership in the various charches of this city all who have been brought in during these score or more of "awakenings," and the sacramental army here would lose many of its ablest officers, with hundreds of the most laborious in the ranks. Rochester has become what it is religiously very largely through the agency of revivals.

THE BIBLE.

The Monroe County Bible Society was formed in this city March, 1821; L. Ward, M.D., president. At its fourth anniversary a resolution was adopted to place a copy of the Sacred Scriptures in every house of the county — a plan afterwards responded to by the parent society with reference to the entire land. One of our citizens contributes his $1,000 annually, and others very considerable sums. Rochester is now and has ever been a cheerful and abundant sustainer of the American Bible Society and the American and Foreign Bible Society (Baptist). Present depository of American Bible Society, 75 State street.

FOREIGN MISSIONS.

Rochester has had, during the last forty years, representatives of both sexes in many continents and islands beyond the sea, while its christian citizens have contributed largely to sustain various missionary societies. Among the earlier missionaries were Rev. Messrs. Green, Comstock, Cherry, Ward, Hunt, and Mrs. Bishop (Stone), Smith (Chapin), DeForest (Sargent), McKinney (Nelson), &c.

TRACTS AND BOOKS.

Monthly tract distribution commenced here at an early day, and has been continued with greater and less regularity to the present time. At the depository of the American Tract Society, on State street, D. Grosvenor, superintendent, and upon the shelves of the various book stores, may be found the rapidly appearing issues of the various Boards, etc., of publication, representing all aspects of religious doctrine and ecclesiastical polity. Two weekly religious papers were for several years published here, viz: Rochester Observer, edited by the late Samuel Chipman; and Genesee Evangelist, by Rev. A. G. Hall, D. D., and subsequently by the late Rev. R. W. Hill; with other journals more limited in the number of readers and area of influence.

SABBATH SCHOOLS.

The youth of Rochester have always received a large amount of mental and religious attention. If they do not make good citizens and become exemplary christians, the fault will be their own. Each Lord's day sees large rooms, in church and chapel, filled with children of all ages and social relations, receiving instruction from well qualified and faithful teachers who willingly forego their own rest that they may engage in the voluntary labor of love. The first Sabbath school was organized in the summer of 1818, under the direction of Messrs. Peck, Scofield, and others, but suspended during winter. In 1822 much interest was awakened by a visit from that "apostle of Sabbath schools," Rev. Thaddeus Osgood. The instruction was largely secular, and all distinctive views of doctrine carefully avoided. In 1825 the schools came under their respective denominations. In 1826 the Monroe County Sunday School Union was formed, and monthly concert on second Monday of each month established. The Genesee S. S. Union was formed in 1827; Josiah Bissell, president, and the late L. B. Tousley (a name to be mentioned with esteem and gratitude) acted as general agent. A depository was established, with L. A. Ward as depositary and treasurer. The Rochester City S. S. Union embraces thirty schools of Protestant denominations, with an aggregate of 996 teachers and 8,648 scholars. The present officers are, president, Thomas Dransfield; secretary, A. H. Cole.

TEMPERANCE.

Rochester took an early part in organized efforts at suppressing the sale and use (as a beverage) of inebriating liquors. "The first public resolutions ever adopted on the principle of total abstinence were passed by the Ontario Presbytery, in a session at Rochesterville, in August, 1827."—(*O'Reilly's Hist.*, *p.* 100.) The first mayor of the city of Rochester, Hon. Jonathan Childs, in 1834, resigned his office rather than sign licenses to sell spirituous liquors. Rev. Dr. Penny, when on a visit to his native Ireland, was instrumental in organizing the first efforts for suppressing the use of intoxicating liquors in that land. Aristarchus Champion, Esq., met the entire expenses of Mr. Chipman, who, during 1833-4 travelled 4,400 miles, visiting all the penitentiaries, jails and poor houses in the State to secure facts and disseminate information upon this subject. Colonel A. W. Riley spent two years in Great Britain lecturing to crowds upon total abstinence. Rev. Dr. F. DeW. Ward edited the first paper in any language of India devoted to the cause of total abstinence. The present city associations in advocacy of the cause of total abstinence, as a beverage, from all that intoxicates are, Independent Order of Good Templars, five lodges, Sons of Temperance, Cold Water Temple, Rochester Temple of Honor.

FIRES.

The church edifices destroyed by fire have been the First Methodist, Bethel (now the Central Presbyterian), Second Baptist, Saint Paul's, Unitarian, Associate Reformed, Saint Peter's (Presbyterian), Lake Avenue, Third Presbyterian, Christian where Plymouth church now stands, German Evangelical subsequently rebuilt, and First Presbyterian injured beyond repair. In most instances others have been erected more commodious and imposing. Among the present ecclesiastical structures a leading place belongs to the Saint Patrick's, Saint Peter's (Pres.), Third Presbyterian, Second Baptist, Brick, Central, Plymouth, with First Presbyterian, First Baptist, and Calvary now in course of erection.

BENEVOLENT AND CHRISTIAN INSTITUTIONS.

Female Charitable Society.—Organized 1822. President, 1871, Mrs. Maltby Strong.

Home for the Friendless.—Organized 1849. President, 1871, Mrs. Selah Matthews. Building on East avenue, corner Alexander street.

Orphan Asylum.—Organized 1837. President, 1871, Mrs. Lysander Farrer.

Church Home of the Protestant Episcopal Church of Rochester.—Organized 1868. President, 1871, Mrs. George H. Mumford.

UNIVERSITY OF ROCHESTER.

President—Martin B. Anderson, LL.D.

Professors—Asahel C. Kendrick, D.D., A. Judson Sage, S. A. Latimore, A. H. Mixer, J. F. Quinby, LL.D., J. H. Gilmore, Henry A. Ward, and Otis H. Robinson. Students, 121.

ROCHESTER THEOLOGICAL SEMINARY.

President and Theological Professor—Rev. E. G. Robinson, D.D.

Professors—Rev. Horatio B. Hacket, Rev. J. W. Buckland, D.D., Rev. George H. Whittemore, and Rev. Augustus Rauschenbush (in the German department). Students, 71.

RAPID CHURCH ERECTION.

The Third Presbyterian church and the Court street church were erected, the former in one week and the other in one month from the time in which the trees were standing in the forest. Josiah Bissell, Esq., and Colonel A. W. Riley were the executive officers in these rapid movements. The buildings stood for many years, and answered their purposes completely.

FALL OF A STEEPLE.

When Saint Paul's was erected the spire was to be two hundred and twenty-seven feet in height. All went on hopefully, but, alas, without success. It was mid-day. Providentially the twenty or more workmen were at their homes. A gust came careening from the west. For a few moments it met the attack nobly. A second onset, fiercer than the former, was too much, and the stately column fell back upon the roof, injuring nothing but the building, and leading to a change in the finish above the tower.

THE END.

www.ingramcontent.com/pod-product-compliance
Lightning Source LLC
Chambersburg PA
CBHW020243170426
43202CB00008B/209